Horrid Laughter in
Jacobean Tragedy

Horrid Laughter
in Jacobean Tragedy

Nicholas Brooke

BOOKS
10 East 53d St. New York 10022
(a division of Harper & Row Publishers, Inc.)

Published in the U.S.A. 1979 by
HARPER & ROW PUBLISHERS, INC.
BARNES & NOBLE IMPORT DIVISION
ISBN 0-06-490701-5
LC 79-53305

British Library Cataloguing in Publication Data

Brooke, Nicholas
Horrid laughter in Jacobean tragedy.
1. English drama–17th century–History
and criticism
2. English drama (Tragedy)–History and
criticism
I. Title
822I.05I   PR658.T7

Printed in Great Britain

Contents

for

Kate Holden

'And in this flea, our two bloods mingled bee'

Preface

A few years ago I took a seminar in the University of East Anglia entitled 'Jacobean Tragedy' and found that my students were unready to accept the presence of serious laughter in plays which they wanted to discuss in the pseudo-Aristotelian terms which have been customary with us since the nineteenth century; they either denied the laughter or, where it was patent, deplored it. The next time I taught the subject I titled the seminar 'Horrid Laughter' and was taken aback by an opposite response: that time the students saw the laughter so clearly that they wanted to discuss the plays as comedies and were only with difficulty persuaded to recognise the tragic context. Those experiences affected the form of this book: I do indeed want to affirm and discuss the peculiar presence and kinds of laughter which both directors and critics have usually undervalued and sometimes denied; but I want to do that with a clear sense of the pain and violence the plays so powerfully present, and of the moral and social contexts in which they are located. In other words, my ambition is at one and the same time to argue for a change in our perception of the plays and to connect that with what is already generally understood. It follows that by no means all the book is about laughter at all.

I hope therefore that this book will interest anyone who

knows the plays already, and be able also to serve as a useful introduction for those who do not, and I share the ambition of any critic of plays to be useful to those who revive them on the stage.

My largest debt, accordingly, is to productions I have seen or been involved in. After them, it is certainly to the editors of the *Revels* editions of the plays, R. A. Foakes, John Russell Brown, N.W. Bawcutt, J. R. Mulryne and Derek Roper, for the quality of their texts (which I have used for all quotations) and for the lively interest of their commentaries and introductions; but since these editors are all known to me personally, and some are close friends, I should perhaps state that I know they will often disagree with me and that they are in no way to blame for my opinions. I owe much too, of course, to many other writers on the plays whose work is acknowledged in the notes and bibliography. Years ago Lorna Sage and Victor Sage were students when I was at Durham; they are now my colleagues, and it has sometimes seemed as if they identified my sense of humour with this subject: I think they are wrong, but am happy to acknowledge here my huge debt to their conversations about this and many other topics. I owe much too to the students in the seminars I have described. To turn these ideas into a book I needed the friendly persuasion of Helen Fraser, then of Open Books, and I was given the opportunity to develop them in lectures to the University of Birmingham Summer School at Stratford upon Avon in 1977 and 1978 by its Directors, Dr Gareth Lloyd Evans and Professor David Palmer. Some have also been delivered in the University of East Anglia. Lectures have been criticised as one-way communications, but to the lecturer they seldom seem so for he learns from, and is sometimes encouraged by, the collective response of an audience as well as individual comments. Out of those lectures this book has finally grown.

Harwood-in-Teesdale and Norwich, autumn 1978

I

Laughter in Tragedy

Direct human registration of emotion is not, in truth, much wider than that of any other animal: we laugh, and we cry. Those two, and those two alone, are universal signs and universally understood. Truly we can also smile and frown, but they are stages towards laughter and tears, and for the rest of the grimaces of the most expressive face we need conventions, a language, to interpret them: they are not universal. What follows from this is that either extreme, laughter or tears, covers a very wide range of actual emotion, and neither can be usefully reduced to a single definition; yet the registrations are so definite that we do tend to generalise. Dramatic tears have been richly documented in the critical discussion of tragedy over the past 150 years, born in the work of Hegel and Nietzsche; yet literal tears have been categorised as 'pathos' and accorded a secondary position. There has been much less discussion of laughter: only two classic studies receive regular attention, Freud on Jokes and Bergson on Comedy (1). Freud's work is not, to my mind, among his most interesting: he meant literally 'jokes', chiefly funny stories but also practical jokes; he wrote in an age peculiarly given to joking, as he was himself, but he does not seem to have recognised it as peculiar. He is interesting about the triggers of particular laughs, but to the study of laughter as a whole it is no more than a side-line. Bergson is richer and much more subtle. He warns against reducing laughter to a single form, yet his theory does seem to do that, as theories will, however varied the modes he considers. He sees laughter as essentially normative, a social correction to any forms of social abnormality, and he insists that that is not necessarily, perhaps not even commonly, a good thing. Such normative comedy destroys indiscriminately the eccentric, the original, the individual, and may therefore be very undesirable. I recognise the existence of his kind of laughter, and his study is a superb analysis of it, but it still limits the range of the subject and so contributes to confusion about it. His theory ignores, to take only one instance, the laughter that celebrates anarchy or generates chaos, and in either sense is totally hostile to any normative process.

I am making this argument to clear away prejudice about what is funny and what is not, or what may constitute proper or improper laughter in any kind of play. I think its forms are infinitely varied, and need independent thought wherever they occur. To some, laughter is always 'nice clean fun'; to others it seems always to have an element of cruelty; neither proposition seems to me in the least true. There *is* such a thing as the laughter of pure delight: lovers laugh when they meet in public, and they laugh privately in bed together. Their laughter *may* emerge into scorn for the dull people around, or contempt for the conventions that deny to others the freedom in love-making that they enjoy; but it does not necessarily do either: it is, essentially, pure delight. At the other extreme, I suppose, is the brutal jeering laughter of triumphant sadism enjoying the torture and destruction of a victim–a nightmare of complicit participation in which even the normally gentle will occasionally find themselves, disgustingly, involved. Shakespeare reaches towards the laughter of delight in his romantic comedies – *A Midsummer Night's Dream* or *As You Like It* for instance, or even *Twelfth Night* – however much of irony or ambiguity they have as well; and he displays the brutal laughter when the Empress's sons rape and mutilate Lavinia in *Titus Andronicus*, or when Achilles and his Myrmidons butcher Hector in *Troilus and Cressida*, or when Hamlet bullies Ophelia towards a brothel-nunnery.

I have offered laughter, so far, as an absolute opposed to tears; in fact, even more bafflingly, it is not a perfect absolute. Beyond it, for one thing, is the horrible paralysis of hysteria; and the truth is that hysteria is a felt presence in a great deal of actual laughter which can often be far more disturbing than relaxing. For another thing, these opposites of laughter and tears easily and bewilderingly transpose into each other: it is notorious that at funerals, after weeping at the grave, we become edgily jokey at the baked-meats; equally, the delight of reunion with someone we are really fond of is often absurdly expressed in tears. Such instances can easily be multiplied and like either registration alone, laughter or tears, they range over a multiplicity of emotional conditions and tones irreducibly different from each other. It is not that one is more extreme than the other, but that either in extremity tends to turn into the other.

This is certainly one point at which the subject relates importantly to tragedy. Tragedy deals in extreme emotions, not all of the same kind: death, suffering, heroism, torture, cruelty, nobility, horror, and so on. And because they are extreme, they are all *liable* to turn over into laughter. It is not surprising that there have been strenuous efforts to resist that tendency, and we still suffer from the inhibiting effects of a tradition that goes back at least to French classicism in the seventeenth century, requiring their absolute separation: any laughter at the denouement of a tragedy is in bad taste, and when it breaks out (as it often does) is felt to be a disaster for the dramatist, actors, production–and the audience, who mutter 'sh! sh!' to each other, and feel they have been cheated of the emotional climax they have been brought up to expect. The English tradition, as Sidney noted with disgust and

Dryden with puzzled approval, has always resisted the separation. Shakespeare is known to move us more deeply than any other dramatist, but his greatest tragedies all contain powerful comic elements, mostly related to clowning. Dryden invented the term 'comic relief', but it has been long accepted that that is quite inadequate: Lear's Fool should be funny if he can, but his jokes do not relieve – they aggravate the tension. The Gravedigger in *Hamlet* is lighter, but he is light about death, just as Macbeth's Porter is about Hell. And so on; but the laughter gets closer still to the central figures: Hamlet is himself a grim joker, sometimes close to a clown, and Lear becomes his own painful fool. Brutus fumbles his suicide in a way that threatens laughter; so does Antony, whose clumsy loss of dignity extends into his death when Cleopatra has so much trouble hoisting the heavy body onto her monument.

All this we have become accustomed to accept, on one condition, that the end is purely solemn. Antony, in *Julius Caesar*, redeems Brutus in his splendid encomium 'This was the noblest Roman of them all'; and in *Antony and Cleopatra* he finally restores his own linguistic splendour with 'I am dying, Egypt, dying' which is endorsed by Cleopatra's marvellous speech over his dead body. The muddle and rush of Hamlet's last duel can invite laughter (and very likely should), but it is silenced by his dying fall: 'Absent thee from felicity awhile', and by Horatio's 'Good night, sweet prince,/And flights of Angels sing thee to thy rest!' Whatever dangerous thoughts have opened up, the conclusion is, or seems to be, unalloyed emotional satisfaction. I have never heard of laughter at the end of *King Lear*.

By force of Shakespeare's familiarity we are conditioned to expect similar conclusions from his contemporaries (as well as to simplify, often enough, his own endings). Some of them, Chapman especially, do provide them; it is the more remarkable that most do not. There is a line from Marlowe and Kyd at the beginning of Shakespeare's career, through Marston to Tourneur and Webster, and on to Middleton and Ford just after Shakespeare's death, of great plays that are unquestionably tragedies though they rather exploit than silence the relation of tears to laughter.

The forms this can take vary considerably, of course, and I want to look at several, but one that is recurrent most clearly identifies the issue. It springs from the celebrated *The Spanish Tragedy*, first performed in the late 1580s. Kyd's play is highly formalised, setting out a complex analysis of the workings of revenge in both public and private patterns. It begins with war, which, however supposedly licensed as honourable killing, provokes revenge and leads on to murder and so by progression to the final multiple deaths. Its dramatic modes range in remarkable variety from the extensive solemnity of the opening, through the ironic macabre humour of the hired murderer Pedringano boasting of his expected reprieve even while he is being executed, to the straightforward madness of the victim's mother, to the far more complex strains of Hieronimo's cracking mind, the good judge who finds no relief in justice and so resorts to his own manic but sane revenge for his murdered son and mad wife. His plan involves all the principals in a totally stylised court entertainment where the mimetic deaths all turn out to be 'real', and the presenter ends by tearing out his own tongue before it can betray secrets he has already eloquently revealed. The play is solemn, violent, horrid, grotesque, ironic, tragic, absurd. You may call it all of those, but what you cannot do is to single out any one and suppress the rest. If it is not horrid it is not absurd; and its kind of tragic perception depends on seeing the grotesque ironies. What it certainly is, is stylised: in the end, a kind of dance of death. In recent theatre, ballet companies have enacted such scenes for us; because dance has been divorced from drama, we judge them primarily in terms of movement, but not exclusively. Drama is commonly assumed to be more naturalistic, and Kyd can do that impressively, but overall stylisation of language and action so marked as his approximates towards dance.

Shakespeare imitated much from *The Spanish Tragedy* in *Titus Andronicus*: the complex shifts from psychological shock to grim joke, to physical horror (rape and mutilation), and the manic devising that ends in a show – serving the Empress with a stew made out of her own sons. It, too, depends on a difficult oscillation between naturalism and stylisation, but it does not actually end with a formal masque-dance: Shakespeare relies on the verbal stylisation of emblematic punishments for Aaron and Tamora, exposed to the natural world they have affronted. *Titus* was very early in Shakespeare's career and he never exactly repeated the form; but much of what baffles critics of *Hamlet* derives from that tradition.

Marston's *Antonio* plays oscillate between tragic rhetoric and blatant farce, moral *sententiae* and apparent self-parody. They obviously owe a great deal to the line I am discussing, and, for Tourneur at least, presumably contributed significantly to what followed; but I confess myself baffled as to what they are in themselves, he seems so little committed to the violence he presents. Tourneur's *The Revenger's Tragedy* outdoes Kyd in grotesque stylisation: two sets of masquers follow each other in the last act to kill the same set of victims, so that the second set stab bodies that are already dead; it can be very eerie, and grotesquely funny as well. Webster's two tragedies, *The White Devil* and *The Duchess of Malfi*, are full of elaborate 'set pieces' (The Arraignment of Vittoria, the dumb show in the Cathedral at Ancona, the masque of madmen before the Duchess's murder, etc.), but they do not actually end in stylised dances. Nor does Middleton's *The Changeling*, but his only other tragedy, *Women Beware Women*, does: virtually the entire cast are at a banquet watching a masque in which the actors wilt and die of poisons they have served each other; and the engineer of this grotesque entertainment is caught in his own trap operated by his idiot-nephew, so that he disappears hilariously/horribly from sight down a trap-door onto spikes below. Ford's *'Tis Pity She's a Whore* also ends in a banquet; there is no masque there (though there is one at the beginning of act IV), but something like one in stylisation when the hero arrives with the heart of his sister/lover displayed on his dagger.

There the line ends: Ford's later plays are very different in form and tone. There it ends, but Kyd is not strictly where it began: Kyd constructed with remarkable originality, but out of a long established tradition. It is still common to offer Jacobean tragedy as a sort of amazing decadence from an imaginary condition of 'serious' tragedy before, so it is important to stress that that never existed in English. The form of Shakespearian ending which I discussed was, in its time, the exception, not the rule. Before Marlowe and Kyd, *English* tragedy (apart from one isolated academic experiment, *Gorboduc*) was largely violent moral farce. It emerged from late medieval morality plays where sardonic humourists mocked and derided the solemn morals with strikingly ambivalent results (2). In that tradition, any pretensions of humanity to secular glory (Kingship, etc.) were seen as farcically evil. In the mid-sixteenth century Cambises starts his play as ruler of Persia, conquers Egypt, returns home to become an outrageous tyrant who spends his time outdoing his own barbarity until he finally succeeds in killing himself–not as deliberate suicide, though it is by his own act. That is ingeniously perfect as a moral conclusion, but that is not all: the play is stage-managed by the Vice, Ambidexter, whose witty-destructive commentary makes everybody, good and bad alike, absurd.

All this springs, not from a crudity of imagination, but from a radically unfamiliar valuation of the human image in art: it is seen as small, trivial, weak; at best pathetic, at worst feeble. The beautiful bodies of the Italian renaissance were either unknown or repudiated, the grandeur of Michelangelo's Adam altogether alien. 'Greatness' was evil, whether in splendour or in cunning – Satanic either way (and later aligned with Machiavelli). To make tragedy you must make images of heroic stature, and that means turning the image upside down, to see in bad men, not virtue of course, but virtú–the dynamic quality by virtue of which a man has the energy of superiority; the bloody tyrant has to become *also* imaginative visionary. That is what Marlowe did with Tamburlaine: like Cambises, he is a bloody-minded thug with a very nasty sense of humour, but wholly unlike Cambises, Tamburlaine is also a superb imaginer of world-power. Marlowe's plays are still tragi-farces, but he gives them a wholly new dimension of magnificence and thus creates a new ambi-valence – admirable, *and* evil. *The Jew of Malta* is marvellous farce, but with an imaginative dimension that gives it, at times, a most disturbing impressiveness; and the Jew ends in a mocking echo of the end of such as Cambises, by falling into the boiling cauldron (traditional image of hell-mouth) which he had constructed for an enemy. *Dr. Faustus* is more obviously a tragedy: the final speech is one of the most intense in English drama, and it is without a hint of laughter; but the process by which the play arrives at that includes repeated shifts into the wild comedy of human absurdity and triviality.

The tradition of English tragedy, then, springs from violent farce, and makes its heroes directly out of con-ventional images of evil. To that they were returned when Milton drew on Marlowe and the Jacobeans for his ex-traordinary image of Satan in *Paradise Lost*. From that tradition Shakespeare moved aside, partly; none of his heroes is unequivocally virtuous, and two, Richard III and Macbeth, are explicitly evil; Richard indeed is a joker who notes his own relation to the morality play Vice. Of the others, Othello and Antony are at once magnificent and rotten, and Horatio might have done better to describe Hamlet as a sweet and sour prince. But the point I want to make is that the plays this book is concerned with, though they often echo Shakespeare (especially the sardonic humour of *Hamlet*) are not failed plays of his kind: they are in a different mode, and can only be understood when that mode is understood. In none of them is there a final repudiation of farce: they end, again and again, with the grandeur and the grotesquerie simultaneously perceived, tears and laughter equally projected. They have, I think, been most often mutilated by conventional expectation of hushed tragic dignity, so that they are nearly always cut as well as directed with care to make the audience feel that if it laughs it is guilty, so that when it does (as it always does) it seems to dismiss the play instead of participating in it.

II

The Revenger's Tragedy

Tourneur's first play obviously owes a great deal to
Marston. Marston was satiric, violent, comic, tragic,
romantic, parodying and self-parodying by turns, and in
consequence oddly detached, objective even if we cannot
be quite sure what the object was. His languages include
the sententious and the savage; he was a moralist and an
ironist. So, no doubt, was Tourneur; but Tourneur's
intensities connect more powerfully. I almost wrote
'consistently', but if that implies any clearly statable
consistency, then they do not have it. Moralist criticism (1)
searched the play for its positives, and doubted if they were
there. An earlier tradition, in the late nineteenth century,
searched the play for its author and often doubted if he
were there, but when they did find him, found a violent,
life-hating, bitter cynic – of genius. His later play, *The
Atheist's Tragedy*, has much of the same quality, generally
less intense, and it combines it with the most explicitly
Christian plot of any Jacobean play. So Tourneur was an
orthodox Christian, and there is no reason to suppose he
underwent a conversion between the two plays. The
explicit Christian conclusion of *The Atheist's Tragedy* can
be fitted to *The Revenger's Tragedy*, and nothing will
contradict it; indeed, in act V, an ominous comet and a
crash of thunder are powerful reminders of powers beyond

the human world of corruption and disaster. In *The Atheist's Tragedy* the defeated atheist acknowledges finally that there is a power above Nature, but in *The Revenger's Tragedy* the resolution is not so clear and certainly not so articulate. The affirmation of supernatural power is there, but it may be absorbed in the ironic context, as Vindice's words suggest:

> Mark, thunder! Dost know thy cue, thou big-voic'd
> cryer?
>
> (V.iii.42)

That parodies the ominous rhetoric of the epic tradition, and it also echoes Hamlet's ironic edgy jokeyness about his father's ghost in the cellarage. The fact is that Hamlet's ironic response to a profoundly disturbed world provided a language, a tone, a perception that dominates a great deal of the writing of both Tourneur and Webster. It belongs to the early seventeenth century, and it contains certainly a hostility to illusion, a disturbed recognition that the Elizabethan golden world was a myth and not a reality. But it is a crude error to attribute this to distaste for the notorious corruption of James I's court: Shakespeare wrote *Hamlet* about 1600, and Marston's *Antonio's Revenge* appeared in 1602; the date of *The Revenger's Tragedy* is uncertain (it was printed in 1607), but if it was written after James came to the throne, it must have been very soon after. The disillusion reached London before James; it was his difficult inheritance, not his fault.

The range of the play is made immediately explicit in Vindice's long (49 lines) and brilliant opening speech. He acts as presenter while the main figures of the Ducal Court cross the stage in dumb pageantry:

> Duke; royal lecher; go, grey-hair'd adultery;
> And thou his son, as impious steep'd as he;
> And thou his bastard, true-begot in evil;
> And thou his duchess, that will do with devil.
>
> (I.i.1–4)

So far it is fairly conventional on evil; the language becomes far more alert in the image of the skeleton:

> Four excellent characters–O, that marrowless age
> Would stuff the hollow bones with damn'd desires,
> And 'stead of heat, kindle infernal fires
> Within the spendthrift veins of a dry duke,
> A parch'd and juiceless luxur.   (5–9)

That makes a prelude to the second movement of the speech, which is addressed to the skull he carries with him:

> Thou sallow picture of my poison'd love,
> My study's ornament, thou shell of death,
> Once the bright face of my betrothed lady,
> When life and beauty naturally fill'd out
> These ragged imperfections,
> When two heaven-pointed diamonds were set
> In those unsightly rings–then 'twas a face
> So far beyond the artificial shine
> Of any woman's bought complexion,
> That the uprightest man (if such there be
> That sin but seven times a day) broke custom,
> And made up eight with looking after her. ...
> But O, accursed palace!
> Thee when thou wert apparel'd in thy flesh
> The old duke poison'd,
> Because thy purer part would not consent
> Unto his palsy-lust; ...   (14–34)

Initially the revelation that the Duke we have just seen had poisoned Vindice's girl-friend because she resisted his lust acts as psychological justification for the violence of the opening lines; but it is important to recognise that psychological justification is of secondary interest: they did not need it, because their dramatic force was their immediate justification. 'Explanations' in the play, of any kind, are frequently offered but they are always partial, and never of the kind that grow into the play's significant point. (Such possible questions as, how long has Vindice been carrying the skull, where is the rest of the skeleton, why wasn't she decently buried? remain quite irrelevant.)

In that speech the grotesque, visible, image of a man talking to the skull of his dead mistress is sharply contrasted with the verbal image of her eyes, 'two heaven-pointed diamonds were set/In those unsightly rings'. 'Heaven-pointed' both because they looked piously to-wards heaven, and because they had been pointed, cut as diamonds are cut, by heaven – just as 'unsightly' means both ugly, and blind: the language in such characteristic passages of Tourneur's verse becomes brilliantly con-centrated. It is also characteristic that Vindice keeps transposing into proverbial morals, also with a witty edge:

> That the uprightest man (if such there be
> That sin but seven times a day) broke custom,
> And made up eight with looking after her.

The varied strains of that speech emerge into three distinctive tones at its conclusion:

> Vengeance, thou murder's quit-rent, and whereby
> Thou show'st thyself tenant to Tragedy,
> O, keep thy day, hour, minute, I beseech,
> For those thou hast determin'd! —   (39–42)

That is the formal declaration of Revenge Tragedy; it leads to an immediate change of tone:

>   —hum, who e'er knew
> Murder unpaid? Faith, give Revenge her due,
> Sh'has kept touch hitherto —   (42–4)

Formal speech transposes into colloquialism, and joke; but joke of a very special kind, ironic and bitter. It is turned on us as Vindice thrusts the skull at the audience:

>   —be merry, merry,
> Advance thee, O thou terror to fat folks,
> To have their costly three-pil'd flesh worn off
> As bare as this —   (44–7)

That will be registered as joke, but it may or may not raise a laugh; if it does, it will be an uncomfortable one, for its humour is precisely the humour of the grinning skull, in marvellously bad taste. Finally there is another abrupt shift, back to proverbs, punning again, on 'great':

> —for banquets, ease and laughter,
> Can make great men, as greatness goes by clay;
> But wise men little are more great than they.   (47–9)

This recurrent proverbialising is strange: it seems to give moral assurance to the dangerous wit, but one proverb hardly supports another, and no wisdom seems to grow from them. You may view it as clutching at straws, or as strictly meaningless; certainly it never enunciates anything like 'the moral of the play'. Yet it is one of the ways in which the play continually insists on moral implications.

It is, in fact, a kind of morality play. Vindice is very much a complex character, but his name is simply allegorical, the Italian for Revenge. So are nearly all the names: the Duke's son and heir is Lussurioso; his bastard, Spurio; Vindice's sister is Castiza (Chastity), and his mother is Gratiana (Grace), and so on. But though orthodox morals are always possible, and very obviously alluded to, attention tends to be drawn away from them into perceptions which, if pursued, would make simple judgements untenable. The two major scenes which make this clearest are those with Vindice's mother and sister, because they are set up to offer unusually clear moral exempla, or to seem to. Vindice gets himself into court by taking employment as Lussurioso's pandar, for which he disguises himself as Piato. It emerges that the lady Lussurioso wants is Castiza; Vindice is outraged, but decides to carry on, assuring himself that it will be an effective test of her virtue, and his mother's. So he appears as Piato, and tries to persuade Castiza to prostitute herself: Gratiana's poverty succumbs, and she undertakes to talk her daughter over – and seemingly fails. That is their first scene, II.i. The other is two and a half acts later, IV.iv:

Vindice and his brother Hippolito, no longer disguised, attack their mother with knives and force a confession and repentance from her; then Castiza enters and horrifies her repentant mother by announcing her obedience, her readiness to play the whore. Gratiana, appalled, argues with her, and Castiza finally announces 'I did but this to try you'.

This small sub-plot is simple, morally clear, and has a happy ending, though the play is designated tragedy. It does not sound very interesting, and in itself would not be at all; yet the scenes have always gained attention: they are well-written and dramatically very effective. The reason, I think, is that attention is continually directed to unexpected perceptions. Initially, Lussurioso's lust for Castiza is identified as more than ordinarily perverse, and as a perversion that was nastily common:

> Then thou know'st
> I'th'world strange lust?
>
> (I.iii.55–6)

He means that he wants, not merely a woman, but Chastity itself; the strange lust is the obsession of the seventeenth and eighteenth centuries with virginity. But Vindice's decision to carry out the project has its own perversity: his rage becomes a kind of excitement:

> We are made strange fellows, brother, innocent
> villains; (170)

delight in the paradox settles him down to a dangerous resolve:

> And yet, now angry froth is down in me,
> It would not prove the meanest policy
> In this disguise to try the faith of both ... (175–7)

The play on 'meanest' makes clear just how monstrously mean the idea is, and calls in question all schemes for moral testing. When II.i opens Castiza, alone on the stage, makes it instantly clear that even this issue is not so simple as demonstration requires:

> Maids and their honours are like poor beginners;
> Were not sin rich, there would be fewer sinners.
> Why had not virtue a revenue? well,
> I know the cause, 'twould have impoverish'd hell.
>   (II.i.5–8)

Chaste she is, but she is also poor; she thinks of money, bitterly, and it is clear too that sin interests her. Yet her virtue holds when her mother's does not; Gratiana belittles virtue:

> Dishonourable act?—good honourable fool,
> That wouldst be honest 'cause thou wouldst be so,
> Producing no one reason but thy will.
> And't has a good report, prettily commended,
> But pray, by whom?—mean people, ignorant people
> ...
> But there's a cold curse laid upon all maids;
> Whilst others clip the sun, they clasp the shades.
> Virginity is paradise, lock'd up.   (146–157)

The line is familiar, but presented with unusual force. Castiza's resistance is dramatically projected *by* her mother's argument. Vindice's dismay at his mother's turnabout transposes into excitement again as he pursues Castiza:

> O, think upon the pleasure of the palace;
> Secured ease and state; the stirring meats,
> Ready to move out of the dishes, that
> E'en now quicken when they're eaten;
> Banquets abroad by torch-light, music, sports,
> Bare-headed vassals, that had ne'er the fortune
> To keep on their own hats, but let horns wear 'em;
> Nine coaches waiting,–hurry, hurry, hurry. (199–206)

He goads Castiza to rage by echoing her own thought:

> why are there so few honest women, but because 'tis
> the poorer profession?   (229–230)

And she, interestingly, sees the dramatic tension of the scene in terms of role-playing:

> I cry you mercy, lady, I mistook you;
> Pray, did you see my mother? Which way went she?
> Pray God I have not lost her.
>
> *Vindice.* [*Aside*]   Prettily put by.
>
> *Gratiana.* Are you as proud to me as coy to him?
> Do you not know me now?
>
> *Castiza.*   Why, are you she?
> The world's so chang'd, one shape into another,
> It is a wise child now that knows her mother! (161–7)

and later:

> Mother, come from that poisonous woman there!
>
> *Gratiana.* Where?
>
> *Castiza.* Do you not see her? she's too inward, then.
>   (239–241)

Vindice's involvement in the scene is too hectic. Role-playing is not a simple matter of putting on an act, it involves partly *becoming* the role: he partly *is* Piato the tempter and his final rage dramatically springs from defeat, whether as moral-seeking son, or as pandar-tempter:

>   O,
> Were't not for gold and women, there would be no
> damnation; Hell would look like a lord's great kitchen
> without fire in't ...   (257–9)

Vindice *needs* sin, for fire and warmth.

Very similar points are made in their other scene, IV.iv. The initial violence of the brothers to their mother is *too* violent; and then the brilliant reversal of expectation when the repentant Gratiana is confronted by the 'obedient' Castiza has a catch to it – that Castiza plays the whore too well. She must do that for the scene to work, for Gratiana

to be really shocked, but that leads to a further perception
about role-playing:

> *Castiza.* Now mother, you have wrought with me so
>   strongly,
>   That what for my advancement, as to calm
>   The trouble of your tongue, I am content.

> *Gratiana.* Content, to what?

> *Castiza.*   To do as you have wish'd me;
>   To prostitute my breast to the duke's son,
>   And put myself to common usury.

> *Gratiana.* I hope you will not so.

> *Castiza.*   Hope you I will not?
>   That's not the hope you look to be sav'd in.
>   (IV.iv.98–105)

The play between salvation in a religious or a mundane
sense catches the bitterness perfectly. Gratiana registers that
Castiza is more than pretending: to play that scene, the
actress must play the whore indeed, which means that
Castiza must discover the whore within herself ('She's too
inward then', as she said to her corrupted mother). The
scene becomes much more interesting than its overt moral,
and Castiza has to be perceived as a woman, not merely as
an allegory: her performance demands thought about role-
playing, not simply about 'being' chaste. Even in Castiza
there is a reflection of Vindice and *his* role-playing, the
moral man overtaken by the roles of revenger and pandar.
That is why Castiza's re-conversion cannot easily convince
her mother, and also why it is expressed in passionately
sensual terms:

> O mother, let me twine about your neck,
> And kiss you till my soul melt on your lips;
> I did but this to try you.   (146–8)

These scenes are not in any ordinary sense funny at all;
yet the sharp perceptions they engender have a positively

witty edge. Behind the moral demonstration the subtle dramatic development (it is almost dramatic necessity, since the scenes would be so flat without it) explores alternative understandings which do not displace the moral, though they render it puerile, for they propose images of experience which threaten to become grotesque. Within these scenes grotesque imagery is purely verbal, and therefore restrained; elsewhere in the play it is enacted, and so becomes both dreadful *and* funny.

The element of monstrous humour was always implicit in Vindice's language from his opening speech, and the grotesque was immediately asserted by his production of the skull. The comic potential first becomes explicit in the trial, condemnation and execution of the Duchess's youngest son, oddly known only as Junior Brother. The trial is the play's first major scene, I.ii. Junior has raped the very respectable wife of the respected Lord Antonio; his judges fear that the Duke will intervene in the course of justice, which the Duchess continually and blatantly demands of him. Surprisingly, he fulfills Ducal dignity and resists her pleas. The judges proceed:

> A rape! why 'tis the very core of lust,
> Double adultery!

Junior Brother.   So, sir.

2. Judge.   And which was worse,
> Committed on the Lord Antonio's wife,
> That general–honest lady. Confess, my lord,
> What mov'd you to't?

Junior Brother.   Why, flesh and blood, my lord;
> What should move men unto a woman else?

>   (I.ii.43–8)

On which Lussurioso comments sententiously:

> O, do not jest thy doom...   (49)

Junior persists in doing so, and his jesting has a dangerous defiance which gives it interest:

Well then, 'tis done, and it would please me well
Were it to do again. Sure, she's a goddess,
For I'd no power to see her and to live;
It falls out true in this, for I must die.
Her beauty was ordain'd to be my scaffold,
And yet methinks I might be easier 'sess'd;
My fault being sport, let me but die in jest.

                                    (60–66)

The judges try to proceed against constant interruptions from the Duchess, until at the very last moment the Duke does intervene:

1. Judge. Let that offender —

Duchess.   Live, and be in health.

1. Judge. Be on a scaffold —

Duke.   Hold, hold, my lord.

Spurio. [*Aside*]   Pox on't,
    What makes my dad speak now?   (81–3)

Junior jesting his doom is always potentially funny; Spurio's 'dad' finally releases the laughter.

Junior's older brothers, Ambitioso and Supervacuo, use the delay in execution to prepare trick and counter-trick, but they are simultaneously engaged in plotting to have their half-brother, Lussurioso, executed; it follows with farcical inevitability that their plots are confused, and their warrant for Lussurioso's death is carried out on Junior, who dies protesting, not his innocence, but his confidence of reprieve in his characteristic jesting defiance. So his brothers are presented, on stage, with his bleeding head which (because they don't look at it) they take to be Lussurioso's. Their scenes verge on camp comedy, very different in tone from Vindice's; their incompetence is easy farce, but here it is brought to bear directly on death. Initially they rejoice, nastily enough:

Officer.   My lords,
  E'en at his last, with pardon be it spoke,
  He curs'd you both.

Supervacuo.   He curs'd us? 'las, good soul!

Ambitioso. It was not in our powers, but the Duke's
                                       pleasure.
  [*Aside*] Finely dissembled o' both sides. Sweet fate!
  O, happy opportunity!
                                (III.vi.49–54)

Then Lussurioso enters, and their bewilderment is comic. It dawns on them at last to lift the cloth and see whose head they are holding:

Ambitioso.   Did we dissemble?

Supervacuo. Did we make our tears women for thee?

Ambitioso. Laugh and rejoice for thee?

Supervacuo. Bring warrant for thy death?

Ambitioso.   Mock off thy head?

Supervacuo. You had a trick, you had a wile, forsooth!

Ambitioso A murrain meet 'em, there's none of these wiles that ever come to good. I see now, there is nothing sure in mortality, but mortality. (83–90)

They are a comic duo, but they did mock off his head, and the laughter generates, even from Ambitioso, sudden startling perception.

The peculiar lightness of that scene functions almost as parody of the grotesque scene immediately before it, the murder of the old Duke. Vindice-as-Piato has agreed to extend his pandaring to Lussurioso's father, and bring him a woman in the garden. He is getting steadily more secretive as his roles develop and even his brother does not know who he is providing; his wild excitement is obvious:

Hippolito. Ay, but where's that lady now?

Vindice.   O, at that word
   I'm lost again, you cannot find me yet;
   I'm in a throng of happy apprehensions.
   He's suited for a lady; I have took care
   For a delicious lip, a sparkling eye.
   You shall be witness, brother.
   Be ready, stand with your hat off.   *Exit.*
                                          (III.v.28–34)

He re-enters with his skull dressed up as a living woman:

Vindice. Madam, his grace will not be absent long.
   Secret? Ne'er doubt us, madam; 'twill be worth
   Three velvet gowns to your ladyship. Known?
   Few ladies respect that! Disgrace? a poor thin shell;
   'Tis the best grace you have to do it well.
   I'll save your hand that labour; I'll unmask you.(43–8)

He does so, and reveals the skull:

Hippolito. Why, brother, brother!

Vindice. Art thou beguil'd now? Tut, a lady can,
   At such, all hid, beguile a wiser man.
   Have I not fitted the old surfeiter
   With a quaint piece of beauty? Age and bare bone
   Are e'er ally'd in action. Here's an eye
   Able to tempt a great man—to serve God . . .   (49–55)

It is obviously grotesque, and obviously ludicrous; but it is
by no means a simple joke, as Supervacuo's and
Ambitioso's almost are: Vindice's tone is edged with
hysteria, and it shifts key very easily into his most
celebrated meditation on life and death which, though still
witty, is not ludicrous at all:

       And now methinks I could e'en chide myself
       For doting on her beauty, though her death
       Shall be reveng'd after no common action.
       Does the silk-worm expend her yellow labours
       For thee? for thee does she undo herself?

Are lordships sold to maintain ladyships
For the poor benefit of a bewitching minute?
Why does yon fellow falsify high-ways,
And put his life between the judge's lips,
To refine such a thing? (69–78)

That, strictly, is still grotesque: for it to work, the wild
laughter that generates its power must be established *first*,
in a sense must be purged, or this could not be responded
to; here we do not laugh, but we are brought to this
peculiar intensity of perception precisely by laughter.

The tone immediately shifts again, to the revenge after
no common action, smearing poison on the skull's painted
lips, and restoring 'her' mask. The Duke's encounter is
wittily conducted through heavy double meanings:

Duke. Piato, well done, hast brought her? what lady is't?

Vindice. Faith, my lord, a country lady, a little bashful at
first, as most of them are; but after the first kiss, my
lord, the worst is past with them. Your grace knows
now what you have to do; sh'has somewhat a grave
look with her, but —

Duke. I love that best; conduct her.

Vindice. [*Aside*] Have at all!

Duke. In gravest looks the greatest faults seem less.
Give me that sin that's rob'd in holiness.

*Vindice.*Back with the torch; brother, raise the perfumes.

Duke. How sweet can a duke breathe? Age has no fault.
Pleasure should meet in a perfumed mist.
Lady, sweetly encounter'd; I came from court,
I must be bold with you. [*Kisses the skull.*] O, what's
this? O!

Vindice. Royal villain, white devil! (133–147)

It is grotesque in the extreme; made out of the imagery of
Vindice's speech, it is effectively a dramatisation of his

imagination. The application is morally perfect, and therefore brilliantly witty; it becomes horridly funny. But the laughter is still reversible: when the Duke begs Hippolito to call 'treason' he obliges, and *stamps* on the dying body, which is suddenly not funny at all. Finally, the Duchess and Spurio, whose affair is unknown to the Duke, appear with loud music on their way to a private banquet; as a final torture, a revelation that he can still feel personal jealousy, the brothers prop the Duke up and force him to watch as he dies.

By this point the opposed possibilities of laughter and horror are both fully established. But paradoxically they hardly seem to be opposed: they are so closely allied that laughter becomes the only possible expression of the horror, not, in any possible sense, a relief. It is always of Vindice's kind, horrified laughter, the cackle of skulls. But for actual audience response it is not fully predictable: they may laugh at one moment, go quiet at another–and then with another performance another audience may reverse the sequence or altogether change the rhythm. Whichever you do, laugh or weep, the horror remains. The grotesque at this intensity is a very strange experience: it becomes a mode of perceiving, and reveals a great deal of our response to death, and indeed to life as well, that normally remains decently obscure. Revulsion *and* fascination meet in a very nasty joking.

The pattern of that scene is characteristic of the play. Again and again superb dramatic scenes are exploited at once for their realisation of shock and of laughter, and the play moves back and forth between those polarities so that you often do not know which response dominates. There are moments that are unequivocal; when laughter seems most remote, a crashing bathos will recall it, but most often the tone subsumes both, whether it invites actual laughter or not. This condition affects the structure of the play which as tragedy often seems odd. A careful plot-logic does organise the action but it is not very obviously restrained by probability and seems often too elaborate to be perfectly clear; and when it is clear it is often *too* logical, too neat, to be literally convincing. The neatness undoes the simple morality, but it also serves the sense of comedy, and the structure does work with surprising assurance as comedy: it moves, that is, from scene to scene, focussing perfectly on a series of wildly funny denouements. That is, I think, a very important perception about it: Tourneur was a very accomplished comic dramatist. The evidences of order and control stand in surprising contrast to the sense of wild, barely contained, disorder. Comedy implies containment, detachment, resistance to over-involvement, and the violent perceptions I have analysed work equally powerfully against any such detachment.

This achievement demands ultimate stylisation, hence the aptness of the masquing scenes at the end. Revenge in such general corruption extends beyond the Duke: all his brood of sons and stepsons have also to die, and it is done as a final dance of death—or rather double dance. V.iii begins with a dumb show investiture of Lussurioso as Duke, and proceeds to his banquet. Vindice, Hippolito and two lords dance and kill the four who are sitting at table. Then they leave, after the thunder and a brief dialogue. The other masquers, Ambitioso, Supervacuo, Spurio and a fourth man dance in and drive their swords into the four that are already dead:

> *The* Duke *recovers a little in voice, and groans—calls,* 'A guard! Treason!' *At which, they all start out of their measure, and turning towards the table, they find them all to be murdered.*   (V.iii.48.3–48.6)

Again, the effect is at once weird and funny; you may be horrified, or laugh. The dance measure, once broken, issues in further deaths as they proceed to kill each other, for each had hoped to inherit the dukedom.

That strange double masque is the grand climax of the play; there remains only Vindice's end which is quickly achieved. His delight in revenging has gone far beyond his initial claim for justice into a manic glee in the acts themselves, and he boasts characteristically to Antonio, who has assumed authority and is puzzled by the Duke's death:

> All for your grace's good. We may be bold to speak it now; 'twas somewhat witty carried, though we say it. 'Twas we two murdered him.

Antonio. You two?

Vindice. None else, i'faith, my lord; nay, 'twas well
manag'd.

Antonio. Lay hands upon those villains.　　(96–101)

A witty reversal, which Vindice can,accept wittily:

> Is't come about?

Hippolito.　　　　'Sfoot, brother, you begun.

*Vindice.*May not we set as well as the duke's son?
Thou hast no conscience; are we not reveng'd? ...
'Tis time to die, when we are ourselves our foes.
　　　　　　　　　　　　(106–110)

And so finally:

> 　　　　　　　　We have enough, i'faith;
> We're well, our mother turn'd, our sister true;
> We die after a nest of dukes. Adieu.　　(123–5)

The sardonic self-recognition, still partly ironic boasting, is far more apt than any steadier moral. It is the summary tone for the play's extraordinary accomplishment. It has given maximum dramatic exploration to human perceptions and drives below the conventional surface (Tourneur, even more than Webster, 'saw the skull beneath the skin'). In that it is brilliant; what, beyond that, it leaves behind is the doubtful truth of Castiza, and the far more doubtful omens of comet and thunder.

It makes sense, I think, that Tourneur's later play should offer a religious affirmation so bland that you would expect his irony to destroy it: but its very blandness may be the only response that can be made to such perception, to pull decent clothing over what is exposed and erase the horrid laughter at our own perversity. The quality of the play is precisely in its superb theatricality; the later play *answers* nothing, it simply offers an alternative vision, but it is worth reflection that that reduces its theatrical brilliance. *The Revenger's Tragedy* is not a comedy, though it uses much of the discoveries of comic drama, it is a peculiar and very disturbing kind of tragedy. We do not have to feel deeply for the individuals, not even for the central figure, to feel that: it is a question of the quality of human experience, perceivable as this play makes us perceive it, only through horrid laughter.

III

The White Devil

It is obvious that Vindice is not only the central figure of
The Revenger's Tragedy, but that also his performance, his
language, define its tone. It would be wrong on that
account to narrow it to a study of him: there are very
interesting psychological insights, but they are not central,
nor are they consistent. And many other figures in the
play are also interesting. It deals with a society of sorts as a
reflection of some extreme in the human situation. Vindice
is given a specific social context, of the hard-up gentry, his
family clearly represent genteel poverty, seventeenth
century style. His father died of discouragement
(I.i.119–130), he himself has no employment, his mother
and sister are suffering from poverty. Poverty, therefore,
threatens radically all their moral traditions; the other son,
Hippolito, has a post in the Duke's chamber, and Vindice
is amazed that he can survive in it (I.i.60–61; Hippolito is
an obscure figure, the others are all more clearly defined
than he. Capacity to survive may be his defining feature,
and why his last words accuse his brother of giving them
both away).

Figures akin to Vindice both socially and psychologically, and therefore linguistically, occur in almost all the
plays discussed in this book. Webster adds a characteristic
not in either Tourneur or Middleton: his unemployed

gentry were graduates as well; they have intellectual capacities and training that were expected to fit them for political employment, but all they get is political jobbing. Unemployed graduates were a serious and recognised social problem in the early seventeenth century (1). Graduates or not, all these figures have a distinctive intelligence that makes them caustic commentators and partly reluctant participators in the action: their cynicism is to know about moral values they cannot afford, and their pleasure is in the perversity of their own practice, their relish and disgust at the vices they don't commit, notably lust.

Webster's Flamineo in *The White Devil* and Bosola in *The Duchess of Malfi* are not the central figures in his plays. He shows more interest than Tourneur in the 'Great Men', the dukes and cardinals, inflated monsters who go wearily or violently mad in the moral vacuums their grandeur creates; and he is even more sympathetically interested in the great women. Both his tragedies take their titles from women: Vittoria, the white devil, and the Duchess of Malfi who strangely has no personal name at all. The men are wholly 'grand': in *The White Devil*, the dukes Bracciano and Francisco, in *The Duchess of Malfi* the Duchess's brothers, Duke Ferdinand and the Cardinal; but the women are less exclusive. Vittoria is Flamineo's sister, an impoverished gentlewoman who (unlike Castiza) has secured her position by marriages and possibly began her career, as Monticelso charges, by being a courtesan; the Duchess is an aristocrat who wants a private life and contracts a secret bourgeois marriage with her steward Antonio. Flamineo and Bosola are not plot-wise central then, but they do, like Vindice, have a central influence on the tone and language of the plays (in the original edition of *The Duchess* the cast-list violates normal usage by putting Bosola at the head despite his inferior rank). There is a marked similarity in the sardonic wit of their perceptions about the society around them: they, also, control and define the horrid laughter of their plays. This is perhaps most true of Flamineo; Bosola has much in common with him but is more complex and obscure both in attitude and behaviour, and in *The Duchess* the range of interest is more successfully distributed amongst a range of figures.

Flamineo enjoys his role with little of Bosola's explicit self-disgust, and some of Iago's determined unrepentance. In *The White Devil* only Flamineo and Vittoria generate strong interest for most of the time. Her lover Bracciano is an explosive grandee, his brother-in-law Francisco de Medici is more interesting but not very clearly defined, and Cardinal Monticelso dissociates himself from active malice after he becomes Pope in act IV. All three are prominent in the superb trial scene (III.ii) where their dramatic roles are more clearly defined than elsewhere; it is characteristic of Webster that characters appear changed in some degree, or redefined, in different scenes. Since we have for a long time been used to orienting ourselves in plays by character study, this practice can cause confusion, and it should be said at once that it is not mere dramatic muddle, but changes of perspective governed by dramatic context (2). What people are, or what the significance of their actions is, is not a single decided thing, known and defined, but a mystery emerging into various, not necessarily reconcilable, forms of light. Webster used to be known for his great scenes, but they are not only impressive in themselves, they are impressively varied in their forms, and all emerge from the general dark mist which envelopes his dramatic world. Vittoria, dying, finds

> My soul, like to a ship in a black storm,
> Is driven I know not whither.
>
> (V.vi.248–9)

and her last words are 'O I am in a mist'. Similarly, Bosola in *The Duchess* answers 'How came Antonio by his death?' with

In a mist: I know not how —
Such a mistake as I have often seen
In a play ...

(V.v.93–6)

The mist is a theatrical truth: from it, and from the black storm, emerge brilliant illuminations–diamonds are, as in Tourneur, recurrent images; but they are not all of the same kind, as diamonds indeed are many-faceted.

The White Devil has numerous intimate scenes of dialogue, but it also has a succession of set-pieces such as the dumb-shows of the murders of Vittoria's and Bracciano's spouses watched through a magic glass in II.ii, or the trial scene which was formally headed *The Arraignment of Vittoria* in the original edition, or the weird disguises of Francisco and his gang as Moors, or Bracciano dying inside his poisoned helmet, and so on. (In *The Duchess of Malfi* such scenes are even more varied and more striking.) What it has too much of is a very complicated plot in which one gets lost and in which, I think, the role of Bracciano itself gets lost, as Francisco is in the end entirely lost in his disguise. Complexity of plot is indeed one form of image for the complicated web that entraps people, though here it is not perfectly satisfactory. It should be said however that Webster was no amateur: he wrote only three plays on his own, the two tragedies and a tragi-comedy, *The Devil's Law Case,* but he worked for years both before and after in collaborations where his individuality is remarkably inconspicuous; his experiments were bold, but certainly not the result of inexperience. Against the complexity of plot is set a frequent terseness of utterance which is, by contrast, sharply definitive: Lodovico opens the play with 'Banish'd!' which has a far more general resonance than simply his personal circumstances. Everyone is banished from something, morality, sanity, normality, hope, etc. Similarly, Bracciano's opening words are 'Quite lost Flamineo.' He means he is lost in love for Vittoria, but again the words resonate beyond their immediate application.

Complex plot obviously provides one structure for the play; another depends on the paradox in its title–White Devil–the ambiguity of Vittoria's nature. We are continually prompted to wonder what she is: innocent or devil is the broadest statement of the question, but its possibilities are not all broad, and the reversals become increasingly strange. Her behaviour is repeatedly exposed to interpretation on the stage, and the sharpest interpreter is her brother, but that does not necessarily make him right, nor wrong either. Her initial reluctance to commit adultery he describes as coyness:

> what is't you doubt? her coyness? that's but the superficies of lust most women have; yet why should ladies blush to hear that nam'd, which they do not fear to handle? O they are politic, they know our desire is increas'd by the difficulty of enjoying ...
>
>   (I.ii.17–22)

Flamineo's witty ironies are resolved into commonplace 'wisdom' which betrays its superficiality. Bracciano's violence of feeling may be a great lust or a great love – be, that is, degrading or elevating – or both-at-once. Vittoria's feeling remains masked, it is not even clear if she has any: she may merely be playing a game she cannot afford to avoid.

Yet it is from Vittoria that action proceeds, in a very ambiguous way. Flamineo wittily manoeuvres her husband to lock himself out (Boccaccio-style) and so frees Vittoria to Bracciano. She recounts a dream to him:

> A foolish idle dream, —
> Methought I walk'd about the mid of night,
> Into a church-yard, where a goodly yew-tree
> Spread her large root in ground, ...
>
>   there came stealing in
> Your duchess and my husband, one of them
> A pick-axe bore, th'other a rusty spade,
> And in rough terms they gan to challenge me,
> About this yew.
>
> *Bracciano.*   That tree.

Vittoria.   This harmless yew.
...   Lord how methought
I trembled, and yet for all this terror
I could not pray.

Flamineo. No the devil was in your dream.

Vittoria. When to my rescue there arose methought
A whirlwind, which let fall a massy arm
From that strong plant,
And both were struck dead by that sacred yew
In that base shallow grave that was their due.
                                        (231–255)

Flamineo instantly interprets this as deliberate, fabricated insinuation:

Excellent devil.
She hath taught him in a dream
To make away his duchess and her husband.   (256–8)

It may be so; Bracciano sees it as a fearful woman needing his protective strength:

Sweetly shall I interpret this your dream, —
You are lodged within his arms who shall protect
                                        you,
From all the fevers of a jealous husband,
From the poor envy of our phlegmatic duchess, —
                                        (259–262)

And that it may be too. Cornelia, her mother, overhears her, curses her till she leaves, and so disturbs Bracciano that he holds her responsible for what may follow:

Uncharitable woman thy rash tongue
Hath rais'd a fearful and prodigious storm, —
Be thou the cause of all ensuing harm.   (305–7)

That, too, may be true, because her anger rouses his violence. But if that is true, then Vittoria's dream alone did not rouse it; and if that is so, either her intent failed, or that was not her intent and Flamineo was wrong.

Moving backwards through that labyrinth of suggestions reveals that the telling of Vittoria's dream *could* be
any of the following: pure innocence, retailing a dream
because it happened; more or less unconscious planting of
suggestion; quite conscious planting, though derived from
a genuine dream; or pure fabrication, designed to rouse
Bracciano to action. It could be any of those, or other
possibilities, or, more strangely, some kind of indefinable
amalgam of them all: each is true as you regard it that
way, but the others are true too. Not even the manifest
pun on 'yew' and 'you' will resolve this complexity,
because it can equally be conscious or unconscious for both
of them. Bracciano is at once the powerful protector *and*
manipulated victim; Vittoria is at once frightened woman
and scheming whore. The dramatic achievement is to
expose the many perspectives in the single iconic image,
and to leave them all in place.

A foil to this, strictly its opposite, is the brief but very
effective presentation of Isabella, Bracciano's wife. Technically she has to go through a performance analogous to
Castiza's playing of the whore, revealing an imagination
her 'pure' innocence should not possess. Bracciano, enraged
by Isabella disturbing him in Rome, is confronted by her
perfect affection; the more she does not accuse, the more
angry he becomes–until he curses their marriage:

> accursed be the priest
> That sang the wedding mass, and even my issue.

Isabella. O too too far you have curs'd.

Bracciano.   Your hand I'll kiss, —
This is the latest ceremony of my love,
Henceforth I'll never lie with thee, by this,
This wedding-ring: I'll ne'er more lie with thee.
And this divorce shall be as truly kept,
As if the judge had doom'd it: fare you well,
Our sleeps are sever'd.

>   (II.i.190–198)

Her brother Francisco arrives, and Bracciano expects her to complain to him; she denies that she will:

> No my dear lord, you shall have present witness
> How I'll work peace between you, —I will make
> Myself the author of your cursed vow —
> I have some cause to do it, you have none, —
> Conceal it I beseech you, for the weal
> Of both your dukedoms, that you wrought the
>   means
> Of such a separation, let the fault
> Remain with my supposed jealousy, —
> And think with what a piteous and rent heart,
> I shall perform this sad ensuing part.   (216–225)

And then she plays the part *too* well. Francisco offers a reconciliation with Bracciano:

>   Was your husband loud,
>   Since we departed?
>
> *Isabella.*   By my life sir no, —
>   I swear by that I do not care to lose.
>   Are all these ruins of my former beauty
>   Laid out for a whore's triumph? ...
>
> *Francisco.*   What? turn'd Fury?
>
> *Isabella.* To dig the strumpet's eyes out, let her lie
>   Some twenty months a-dying, to cut off
>   Her nose and lips, pull out her rotten teeth,
>   Preserve her flesh like mummia, for trophies
>   Of my just anger: hell to my affliction
>   Is mere snow-water ...   (235–251)

She goes on to rehearse a prepared speech:

> Sir let me borrow of you but one kiss,
> Henceforth I'll never lie with you, by this,
> This wedding-ring.
>
>   (253–5)

but on the way the dramatic interchange projects from her a jealousy that is more than feigning. Bracciano remains silent, until he *is* reconciled with Francisco in jokey masculine withdrawal from her fury:

> 'Twere best to let her have her humour,
> Some half day's journey will bring down her
> > stomach,
> And then she'll turn in post.
>
> *Francisco.*　　　　　　　　　　To see her come
> To my lord cardinal for a dispensation
> Of her rash vow will beget excellent laughter.
>
> > (272–6)

There is perceptive ambiguity, then, about Isabella; but she remains a devoted wife until she is murdered–and so is the opposite of Vittoria. About her, the ambiguities multiply: Bracciano and his conjuror (magician) see dumb show 'visions' of the murders, in a back room of Vittoria's house; she does not watch, and it is Bracciano not Vittoria who has organised them, employing Dr. Julio and Flaminco. Isabella dies kissing Bracciano's portrait–her murderers have *laughed* as they smeared the poison on, and Camillo's death from a vaulting horse is more obviously hilarious, pointed by Flamineo's comments. Yet Francisco and Monticelso go at once to arrest Vittoria, while Bracciano beats a strategic retreat, protected perhaps by caste solidarity. At that point Vittoria is technically close to total innocence of the crime for which she is brought to trial in III.ii.

Innocence, in fact, is not really the central issue here so much as domination. Monticelso and Francisco are supposed to rule the court, submitting their judgement to the disinterested eyes of the ambassadors; but from the beginning Monticelso's fury is barely under control, and Francisco has to act as moderator. Right at the start he has to handle Bracciano's embarrassing insistence on being present:

Monticelso. Forbear my lord, here is no place assign'd you,
  This business by his holiness is left
  To our examination.

Bracciano.   May it thrive with you.
                         Lays a rich gown under him.
Francisco. A chair there for his lordship.

                                        (III.ii.1–4)

But it is Vittoria who immediately establishes cool superiority:

Lawyer. Domine judex converte oculos in hanc pestem mulierum corruptissimam.

Vittoria. What's he?

Francisco.   A lawyer, that pleads against you.

Vittoria. Pray my lord, let him speak his usual tongue—
  I'll make no answer else.

Francisco.   Why you understand Latin.

Vittoria. I do sir, but amongst this auditory
  Which come to hear my cause, the half or more
  May be ignorant in't.   (10–17)

It is established that she is educated above the norm, even for men. Francisco instructs the lawyer to use English, but his language remains hopelessly fustian–'Why this is Welsh to Latin'–so Vittoria gets him dismissed by Francisco, who proposes to conduct the case himself. But Monticelso loses patience:

  I must spare you till proof cry whore to that;
  Observe this creature here my honoured lords,
  A woman of a most prodigious spirit
  In her effected.

Vittoria.   Honourable my lord,
  It doth not suit a reverend cardinal
  To play the lawyer thus.   (56–61)

It does not; and her retort is still more just when he proceeds to mere abuse:

> This whore, forsooth, was holy.

> *Vittoria.*   Ha? whore — what's that?
>   (77)

He has already been exaggerating; this provokes him to verbal violence about whores:

> Shall I expound whore to you? sure I shall;
> I'll give their perfect character. They are first,
> Sweet-meats which rot the eater: in man's nostril
> Poison'd perfumes. They are coz'ning alchemy,
> Shipwrecks in calmest weather. What are whores?
> Cold Russian winters, that appear so barren,
> As if that nature had forgot the spring.
> They are the true material fire of hell ...   (78–85)

and so on, more and more extravagantly: his words so evidently spring from his own obsessive imagination and not from any evidence about her that Vittoria can respond with perfect effect:

> This character scapes me.
> *Monticelso.* You gentlewoman?
>   Take from all beasts, and from all minerals
>   Their deadly poison —

> *Vittoria.*   Well what then?

> *Monticelso.*   I'll tell thee —
>   I'll find in thee a pothecary's shop
>   To sample them all.

> *French Ambassador.*   She hath lived ill.

> *English Ambassador.* True, but the cardinal's too bitter.
>   (101–7)

He is; and that fact gives her the ascendancy in the scene. She is not *his* 'whore'; but the French Ambassador may still be right that she has lived ill. Whether or not, she can now play with the cardinal's temper to his discredit:

> *Monticelso.* And look upon this creature was his wife.
> She comes not like a widow: she comes arm'd
> With scorn and impudence: is this a mourning habit?
>
> *Vittoria.* Had I foreknown his death as you suggest,
> I would have bespoke my mourning.
>
> *Monticelso.* O you are cunning.
>
> *Vittoria.* You shame your wit and judgement
> To call it so; what, is my just defence
> By him that is my judge call'd impudence?
> Let me appeal then from this Christian court
> To the uncivil Tartar.
>
> *Monticelso.*   See my lords,
> She scandals our proceedings.
>
> *Vittoria.*   Humbly thus,
> Thus low, to the most worthy and respected
> Lieger ambassadors, my modesty
> And womanhood I tender; but withal
> So entangled in a cursed accusation
> That my defence of force like Perseus,
> Must personate masculine virtue—to the point!
> Find me but guilty, sever head from body:
> We'll part good friends: I scorn to hold my life
> At yours or any man's entreaty, sir.
>
> *English Ambassador.* She hath a brave spirit. (119–140)

Challenging the neatly defined roles for men and women – and scorning men – she becomes magnificent, and the English Ambassador is suitably impressed. But it is also felt that he is impressionable, which warns us that though she has put down her accuser, she has not proved her innocence. That is still true when Monticelso goes too far again:

> > I rather think
> 'Twas interest for his lust.
>
> *Vittoria.* Who says so but yourself? if you be my accuser
> Pray cease to be my judge, come from the bench,
> Give in your evidence 'gainst me, and let these
> Be moderators...   (223–8)

Francisco has already admitted that the murder is uncertain
and withdrawn the charge; now Monticelso tries to press
'incontinence' with no better success, and Flamineo can
make the irony overt when the cardinal proceeds to
judgement without having obtained conviction:

> *Monticelso.* ....   here's your sentence, — you are confin'd
> Unto a house of convertites and your bawd —
>
> *Flamineo.* [*aside*] Who I?
>
> *Monticelso.*   The Moor.
>
> *Flamineo.*   [*aside*] O I am a sound man
> > > again.
>
> *Vittoria.* A house of convertites, what's that?
>
> *Monticelso.*   A house
> Of penitent whores.
>
> *Vittoria.*   Do the noblemen in Rome
> Erect it for their wives, that I am sent
> To lodge there?   (263–9)

And finally she can come back with full power:

> *Monticelso.*   Away with her.
> Take her hence.
>
> *Vittoria.* A rape, a rape.
>
> *Monticelso.*   How?
>
> *Vittoria.*   Yes you have ravish'd justice,
> Forc'd her to do your pleasure.   (272–5)

She has not been convicted, so the sentence *is* unjust. Her handling of the scene is superb – and so, therefore, is she: the most impressive *woman* on the Jacobean stage (after Cleopatra). And that remains true whatever degree of innocence or guilt she may actually have. The fascinating truth is that after the trial we *know* about her guilt no more than before, in a sense even less. Her final lines make a claim that is impressive but not a proof of innocence:

> bear me hence,
> Unto this house of — what's your mitigating title?

Monticelso. Of convertites.

Vittoria. It shall not be a house of convertites —
My mind shall make it honester to me
Than the Pope's palace, and more peaceable
Than thy soul, though thou art a cardinal, —
Know this, and let it somewhat raise your spite,
Through darkness diamonds spread their richest light.
>   (286–294)

A triumph so splendid obscures the issue of moral guilt for the larger scope of virtú, Vittoria's power to dominate the men. But Flamineo immediately shifts the perspective to a merely cunning evasion of responsibility for the Duchess's murder, and the change of tone suggests another reading of the whole scene before – that it was all a brilliant act, masking guilt. We simply do not know, now or ever.

Our judgement of Vittoria continues to undergo reversals through act IV, when Bracciano's jealousy in the house of convertites provokes her to renounce him, Flamineo to cynical contempt, and Bracciano to abject penitence:

Flamineo.   A quiet woman
Is a still water under a great bridge.
A man may shoot her safely.

Vittoria. O ye dissembling men!

Flamineo.   We suck'd that, sister,
From women's breasts, in our first infancy.

Vittoria. To add misery to misery.

Bracciano.   Sweetest.
                                           (IV.ii.179–184)

The ambiguity persists in to the long last act. Its first major
concern is the murder of Bracciano, achieved so elaborately that it appears as if it were the grand tragic climax,
though in fact it is completed less than halfway through
the act which in all is nearly twice as long as act IV. The
original text did not mark act divisions, so they may be
misleading (it can't be better divided anywhere else, but
may not be designed for such divisions at all). *The Duchess
of Malfi*, where the original text is divided, puts the
elaborate murder of the Duchess into act IV and destroys
the rest of the cast in act V. The actual proportions are
similar here: Bracciano finally dies, tormented by his
murderers, in the middle of V.iii (the torture is reminiscent
of Vindice's treatment of Lussurioso while he was dying).
Much of the first part of the act is given to disguising,
especially of Florence whose disguise is so perfect it seems
unlikely the audience is expected to penetrate it. His
obsession with revenge leads him to ignore advice to leave
it to others, a curious perception here, as also is his last
affair with Zanche the Moor whose lust is so much
simpler than Vittoria's and so an effective foil for it.
Flamineo is provoked to kill his brother in self-
preservation; but he does it in the presence of his mother
who goes movingly mad. She, like Vindice's family, is the
play's normative conscience, the voice of conventional
Christian morality from which the play departs so far and
so fascinatingly. She provokes another, unexpected, shift of
perspective in Flamineo:

> I have a strange thing in me, to th'which
> I cannot give a name, without it be
> Compassion, ... I have liv'd
> Riotously ill, like some that live in court;
> And sometimes, when my face was full of smiles

Have felt the maze of conscience in my breast.
Oft gay and honour'd robes those tortures try, —
We think cag'd birds sing, when indeed they cry.

(V.iv.113–123)

Flamineo has laughed, but tears are always implicit in the pitch of his laughter, which will again usurp his conscience though not in such a way as to question the emotional truth of this passage. Bracciano wept, but the elaboration of his death brought it near to farce. Now his ghost appears to prelude the play's final movement, when Flamineo concentrates on his sister.

Scene vi opens strangely: Flamineo, in despair and seeking death, horrifies Vittoria by proposing a suicide pact (claiming that he promised this to Bracciano). She resists, but is brought to agree, and he prepares to be shot with suitable rhetoric:

Whither shall I go now? O Lucian thy ridiculous
purgatory! to find Alexander the Great cobbling shoes,
Pompey tagging points, and Julius Caesar making hair
buttons; Hannibal selling blacking, and Augustus crying
garlic, Charlemagne selling lists by the dozen, and King
Pippin crying apples in a cart drawn with one horse.
Whether I resolve to fire, earth, water, air,
Or all the elements by scruples, I know not
Nor greatly care,–Shoot, shoot,
Of all deaths the violent death is best,
For from ourselves it steals ourselves so fast
The pain once apprehended is quite past.

(V.vi.107–118)

This is not impressive, but it is amazingly close to the language he uses 160 lines later, when he actually dies: the effect is of a parody in advance. Vittoria and Zanche fire – and run and tread on him; he ignores that, and sustains his tone despite their contemptuous hostility:

I am mix'd with earth already: as you are noble
Perform your vows, and bravely follow me.

...ria. Whither —to hell? ...

This thy death

Shall make me like a blazing ominous star, —
Look up and tremble. ...

Flamineo. O the way's dark and horrid! I cannot see, ...

(120–138)

But as he works it up to its climax, his rhetoric becomes
increasingly preposterous:

Shall I have no company?

Vittoria.   O yes thy sins
Do run before thee to fetch fire from hell,
To light thee thither.

Flamineo.   O I smell soot,
Most stinking soot, the chimney is a-fire, —
My liver's parboil'd like Scotch holy bread;
There's a plumber, laying pipes in my guts, —it
scalds;

Wilt thou outlive me?

Zanche.   Yes, and drive a stake
Through thy body; for we'll give it out,
Thou didst this violence upon thyself.

Flamineo. O cunning devils! now I have try'd your love,
And doubled all your reaches. I am not wounded:
Flamineo *riseth.*
The pistols held no bullets: 'twas a plot
To prove your kindness to me; and I live
To punish your ingratitude ...   (139–152)

Flamineo rising clinches the increasing suspicion of farce in
the language, and inevitably brings the house down. It's a
brilliantly written scene, always with a comic possibility
that remains uncertain until it is resolved by Flamineo's
revelation. This finally brings out the latent farce in the
whole sequence of absurd disguisings which preceded
Bracciano's death, and brings that forward, here, as the

dominant tone. Flamineo has had this effect recurrently throughout the play—here it seems to be decisive. He and Vittoria both play roles, so effectively that we realise we have never known what they really are.

But of course it is not decisive: Flamineo delivers a diatribe against women, and after her behaviour at his 'death' the case against his sister seems to be confirmed. Then Lodovico and Gasparo burst in to kill them both: the mock deaths are after all to be followed by real death, for both of them. Flamineo's jesting tone remains, but its edge is reversed and it is now sharply serious. Laughter is still a possibility; but our immediate urge to laugh has been exorcised by the mock death, and it is much less likely now; whether or not it happens, we are directed to the intensity within the jests.

Lodovico.   Dost laugh?

Flamineo.   Wouldst have me die, as I was born, in whining?

Gasparo. Recommend yourself to heaven.

Flamineo. No I will carry mine own commendations thither. ...

Lodovico. ...   What dost think on?

Flamineo. Nothing; of nothing: leave thy idle questions, —
I am i'th'way to study a long silence.
To prate were idle, —I remember nothing.
There's nothing of so infinite vexation
As man's own thoughts.   (194–206)

They turn to Vittoria, who this time accepts death as inevitable and resists their squalid bullying impressively, first claiming the right to die before Zanche, and then directly contemptuous of their triumph:

Lodovico.   Strike, strike,
With a joint motion.   [*They strike.*]

Vittoria.   'Twas a manly blow —
   The next thou giv'st, murder some sucking infant,
   And then thou wilt be famous.   (231–4)

And so Flamineo finally reverses his judgement, to articulate the respect that has always been latent in his abuse of his sister:

Vittoria. O my greatest sin lay in my blood.
   Now my blood pays for't.

Flamineo.   Th'art a noble sister —
   I love thee now; if woman do breed man
   She ought to teach him manhood: fare thee well.
   Know many glorious women that are fam'd
   For masculine virtue, have been vicious
   Only a happier silence did betide them —
   She hath no faults, who hath the art to hide them.

Vittoria. My soul, like to a ship in a black storm,
   Is driven I know not whither.

Flamineo.   Then cast anchor. (240–249)

He still sustains his nihilism, most impressively:

   We cease to grieve, cease to be Fortune's slaves,
   Nay cease to die by dying.   ...
   No, at myself I will begin and end:
   While we look up to heaven we confound
   Knowledge with knowledge. O I am in a mist.

Vittoria. O happy they that never saw the court,
   Nor ever knew great man but by report.
                 Vittoria *dies.* (252–262)

After her death he has one last speech; throughout the lines I have quoted there are continual echoes of the mock death scene, now the connection is obvious in the move from proverbial, prosaic history to ironic verse:

   Let all that belong to great men remember th'old
   wives' tradition, to be like the lions i'th'Tower on

Candlemas day, to mourn if the sun shine, for fea.
the pitiful remainder of winter to come.
'Tis well yet there's some goodness in my death,
My life was a black charnel: I have caught
An everlasting cold. I have lost my voice
Most irrecoverably: farewell glorious villains, —

(265–272)

There is, as Flamineo says, some goodness in his death, and in his sister's; its definition is far too subtle to be contained in a term such as stoicism. It depends essentially on the relation here of laughter to tears, and that is superbly controlled; by establishing the parody first, Webster releases the superb mocking courage for its full effect. We laugh and weep at nearly identical language, distinguished by only the slightest shift of tone. On that its unique power to move depends.

. So, in the end, the horror and the laughter are simultaneously focussed, and brilliantly controlled. Earlier, the laughter we might understand was always exceeded by the cheaper laughter that Flamineo invited. In the trial scene, for instance, laughter was always latent, but rarely actual – possibly with Bracciano's antics, certainly with Flamineo's rare asides. But his laugh was purely cynical, ours was more complex: we could laugh with him, but in a different key – just as we can see his cynical view of his sister, but not simply share it. In the end, his laughter adjusts towards ours, so does his view of her, and of death. Vittoria remains, of course, ambiguous: vicious and virtuous, bold and coy, magnificent and cheap. We understand her in the peculiar laughter that establishes her splendour whatever her morals, and thus defines a very powerful response to death and to life. It is difficult to analyse, but it is not difficult to respond to, especially in the theatre. Such laughter is not dismissive, it becomes an essential part, as I have said, of an imaginative mode of perception. To eliminate laughter from the response to death, by stressing exclusively the 'nobility' of tragedy for instance, is to evade an essential knowledge.

IV

The Duchess of Malfi

Webster's second play opens with a scene obviously developed from the opening of *The Revenger's Tragedy*: Antonio, the Duchess's steward, offers a commentary on great figures which is like Vindice's on the Duke and his family, but here they are not confined to dumb-show, each one is extended with brief revealing dialogues. The Cardinal has known Bosola before his time in the galleys, and Ferdinand exposes his manic grandeur more directly to a sycophantic entourage:

> *Ferdinand.* How do you like my Spanish jennet?
>
> *Roderigo.* He is all fire.
>
> *Ferdinand.* I am of Pliny's opinion, I think he was begot by the wind; he runs as if he were ballasted with quicksilver.
>
> *Silvio.* True, my lord, he reels from the tilt often.
>
> *Roderigo, Grisolan.* Ha, ha, ha!
>
> *Ferdinand.* Why do you laugh? Methinks you that are courtiers should be my touch-wood, take fire, when I give fire; that is, laugh when I laugh, were the subject never so witty —
>
> (I.i.116–125)

Ferdinand's laughter is peculiarly chilling, as Antonio comments:

> The duke there? a most perverse, and turbulent
> nature:
> What appears in him mirth, is merely outside;
> If he laugh heartily, it is to laugh
> All honesty out of fashion.   (169–172)

Grotesque laughter is firmly established as a dimension of the play. It takes another form when the Duchess appears with the Cardinal to join Ferdinand: the brothers assert male familial rights over her widowhood which she resists with attempted jokes (her insistent normality exposes the obsessive abnormality of their masculine domination):

> *Ferdinand.*   Marry! they are most luxurious
>   Will wed twice.
>
> *Cardinal.*   O fie!
>
> *Ferdinand.*   Their livers are more spotted
>   Than Laban's sheep.
>
> *Duchess.*   Diamonds are of most value
>   They say, that have pass'd through most jewellers'
> hands.
>
> *Ferdinand.* Whores, by that rule, are precious: —
>
> *Duchess.*   Will you hear me?
>   I'll never marry ...   (297–302)

Ferdinand converts her light jokes into sinister ones:

> *Duchess.* I think this speech between you both was
> studied,
>   It came so roundly off.
>
> *Ferdinand.*   You are my sister —
>   This was my father's poniard: do you see?
>   I'd be loth to see't look rusty, 'cause 'twas his: —
>   I would have you to give o'er these chargeable revels;

> A visor and a mask are whispering-rooms
> That were ne'er built for goodness: fare ye well: —
> And women like that part which, like the lamprey,
> Hath ne'er a bone in't.

Duchess.   Fie sir!

Ferdinand.   Nay,
> I mean the tongue ...   (329–338)

The Duchess cannot impose her tone on that scene; as the brothers leave, she attempts to leave their grotesque world for one of her own making and proceeds to woo Antonio, her steward. Her humour does serve here, and needs to, for he is nervous of responding, and she is nervous at assuming the male role in wooing that her social superiority forces on her. It has often been pointed out that there is here a violation of correct 'order' which is supposed to have affected Jacobean audiences with the moral force of a tragic 'flaw'; technically that might be true, but as William Empson pointed out, the play entirely assumes the audience's complicity and therefore approval of the Duchess's action. The social distinction does, however, relate to another value scheme: the Duchess and Antonio achieve a private domesticity which is implicitly closer to middle class patterns than to the image of aristocracy given in the play. It is the play's most powerful vision of living *virtue,* and can only be vice to the mad vision of the great men, her brothers:

Duchess.   sir, be confident —
> What is't distracts you? This is flesh, and blood, sir;
> 'Tis not the figure cut in alabaster
> Kneels at my husband's tomb.   (452–5)

'Flesh and blood' invites warm support against monumental grandeur, the grotesque commonplace of a seventeenth century widow being sculpted on a tomb while she is still alive. The Duchess's tone is perfect, and her delightful language is the speaking voice of her much commented on beauty: she becomes an aesthetic as well as a moral value – as Bosola perceives in IV.i, commenting on her nobility in prison:

> You may discern the shape of loveliness
> More perfect in her tears, than in her smiles ...
>
> (IV.i.7–8)

Aesthetics, the forms of imagination, become very important in this play: the major scenes are so carefully wrought as to become individual images in sharp contrast to each other, or sometimes transposing into their own opposites (e.g. III.ii). That depends on the awareness of formal art in the structure of the play, where acts are much more significant units than in *The White Devil*, with major time gaps between them (a practice which was more frequent in plays designed for the so-called 'private' houses): between I and II the Duchess gets pregnant; between III and IV she has no less than two more children (her fecundity is continually stressed against the sterility of her brothers); act IV is entirely occupied with her death, and there is a substantial shift of time and place before act V.

As the Duchess progresses in fertility, Ferdinand proceeds into destructive madness; the facts he suspects about her (her family is kept secret an amazingly long time, even from Bosola who is planted in her household to spy on her) are gradually confirmed:

>   Methinks I see her laughing—
> Excellent hyena!—talk to me somewhat, quickly,
> Or my imagination will carry me
> To see her, in the shameful act of sin.

Cardinal. With whom?

Ferdinand.   Happily with some strong thigh'd
>   bargeman;
> Or one o'th'wood-yard, that can quoit the sledge,
> Or toss the bar, or else some lovely squire
> That carries coals up to her privy lodgings.

Cardinal. You fly beyond your reason.

Ferdinand.   Go to, mistress!
   'Tis not your whore's milk that shall quench my
                                                wild-fire,
   But your whore's blood.
                                              (II.v.38–48)

A few lines later the Cardinal asks, 'Are you stark mad?'
(66); mad he is not as yet, but he is moving that way
through nauseated obsession with his sister's sexuality. His
reaction, here, could be described as a dormouse
complex – 'In, in; I'll go sleep' (76); in I.i he instructed
Bosola to be like a politic dormouse (282), but he himself
becomes a compulsive one however much he tries to
maintain it as politic still:

   Till I know who leaps my sister, I'll not stir:
   That known, I'll find scorpions to string my whips,
   And fix her in a general eclipse.
                                              (II.v.77–9)

Antonio comments on the condition at the beginning of
the next scene:

   He is so quiet, that he seems to sleep
   The tempest out, as dormice do in winter ...
                                              (III.i.21–2)

Whatever Ferdinand does becomes grandly conspicuous:
later 'The Lord Ferdinand laughs', now:

Delio.   The Lord Ferdinand
   Is going to bed.   (37–8)

Visual images on the stage are peculiarly powerful in act
III. Scene ii is of a delightful domesticity: idly erotic chat
between Antonio, the Duchess and her maid Cariola. The
Duchess is absorbed in doing her hair before a mirror
(another potential moral, since it is an emblem of vanity,
but again totally harmless as presented), and goes on
happily talking to them while they, to tease her, tip-toe off
the stage:

                                    I prithee,
When were we so merry? — my hair tangles. ...
          Enter Ferdinand [*behind*].
We shall one day have my brothers take you
                                            napping:
Methinks his presence, being now in court,
Should make you keep your own bed: but you'll say
Love mix'd with fear is sweetest. I'll assure you
You shall get no more children till my brothers
Consent to be your gossips: — have you lost your
                                            tongue?
                    [*Turns and sees Ferdinand.*]
'Tis welcome:
For know, whether I am doom'd to live or die,
I can do both like a prince.
                    Ferdinand gives her a poniard.

Ferdinand.   Die then, quickly!
                    (III.ii.52–71)

The reversal from Antonio to Ferdinand projects an instant
switch from life to death, and from wife to prince.
Ferdinand now changes his dormouse for a wolf:

Duchess. Will you see my husband?

Ferdinand.   Yes, if I could change
    Eyes with a basilisk: —

Duchess.   Sure, you came hither
    By his confederacy.

Ferdinand.   The howling of a wolf
    Is music to thee, screech-owl, prithee peace!
    Whate'er thou art, that hast enjoy'd my sister, —
    For I am sure thou hear'st me — for thine own sake
    Let me not know thee: I came hither prepar'd
    To work thy discovery, yet am now persuaded
    It would beget such violent effects
    As would damn us both ...   (86–95)

By the end of the scene he swears never to see her more. The Duchess and Antonio determine to escape as pilgrims to Loretto: yet another potential offence is building up here, the mockery of religion which may also be taken simply as irreligion:

> *Cariola.*   In my opinion,
>   She were better progress to the baths
>   At Lucca, or go visit the Spa
>   In Germany, for, if you will believe me,
>   I do not like this jesting with religion,
>   This feigned pilgrimage.
>
> *Duchess.* Thou art a superstitious fool ...   (313–19)

Her tone is secular, sceptical, and by no means aristocratic. The Cardinal's comment when he hears of it is magnificently ironic and provokes an extraordinarily inverted outburst from Ferdinand:

> *Cardinal.* Doth she make religion her riding-hood
>   To keep her from the sun and tempest?
>
> *Ferdinand.*   That!
>   That damns her: —methinks her fault and beauty,
>   Blended together, show like leprosy,
>   The whiter, the fouler: —I make it a question
>   Whether her beggarly brats were ever christen'd.
>   (III.iii.60–65)

Ferdinand is more than ever a spectacle as he becomes stranger:

> *Pescara.* The Lord Ferdinand laughs.
>
> *Delio.*   Like a deadly cannon ... (54)

It is the same laughter as in act I, but its deadly quality contrasts with the Duchess's flippant blasphemy as hideous danger, not as moral rectitude. Ferdinand's central significance in the play is associated with this horrid laughter, and provides a presence for it lacking in *The White Devil*; that in its turn displaces Bosola in some degree, and accounts

for the different weight his wit has here in comparison
with Flamineo's. Bosola's relationship to Ferdinand and to
the melancholic Cardinal governs the play's tragic perception and accounts for their survival so long after the
Duchess's will to live has been strangled.

Mockery of religion provides the next major visual
spectacle, the elaborate dumb-show in the shrine at
Loretto. It is a splendid ritual, calling for all the spectacular
resources of the theatre (in the finest staging of it I have
seen, at Stratford, Ontario in 1971, the visual splendour
was endorsed by incense released through the air-
conditioning plant; the audience laughed in delighted
admiration, which I take to be precisely the right reaction
to such a baroque tour-de-force.). But the ritual is of the
Cardinal divesting himself of religion and assuming a
soldier's armour. When the Duchess, Antonio and their
children enter it is he, not they, that offends the shrine,
dragging her ring from the Duchess's finger. In the next
scene Bosola arrests the Duchess and in parting from her
husband she realigns herself with at least personal religion
in the celebrated lines

> in the eternal church, sir,
> I do hope we shall not part thus.
>
> (III.v.71–2)

The appeal is far more metaphoric than dogmatic, just as
her marriage was a private avowal:

> I have heard lawyers say, a contract in a chamber
> *Per verba de presenti* is absolute marriage: —
> Bless, heaven, this sacred Gordian, which let violence
> Never untwine.
>
> (I.i. 478–481)

That stands in direct contrast to her brothers' execution of
their personal perversions through constant appeal to the
institutions of Church and State.

The Duchess is therefore isolated for the grotesque
build-up of torture and death in act IV. Ferdinand visits

her in prison but, to keep his vow, in total darkness – and holds out to her what, when the lights come up (candles at the Blackfriars, a verbal illusion presumably at the Globe), turns out to be a dead man's hand. And then more light, and a curtain drawn, reveal the figures of Antonio and the children. The use of theatrical illusion is neat: they seem to be dead bodies, are in fact the live actors posed, *and* can be interpreted as waxworks (they are still alive in fact):

> *Ferdinand.* Excellent: as I would wish; she's plagu'd in
> art.
>
> These presentations are but fram'd in wax,
> By the curious master in that quality,
> Vincentio Lauriola, and she takes them
> For true substantial bodies.
>
> (IV.i.111–15)

There is an echo here of Shakespeare's discussion of Giulio Romano in the last scene of *The Winter's Tale*, but Webster seems to have made this artist up. 'Plagu'd in art' could serve as a motto for the play, for the aesthetics of Webster's work make the fullest use of theatrical art, and only if that is understood can his imaginative perception be grasped. Theatricalism used to be made a criticism of him; in truth it is his excellence.

Aesthetic grotesque, the 'art' of madness, is brought to its climax in IV.ii. Ferdinand's last mad torture is to send in a group of madmen from a hospital to his sister's dungeon. Their performance is organised, as Inga-Stina Ewbank pointed out (1), in the form of an anti-masque as practised in court entertainments. Their antics are funny and obscene, and so are their lines – semi-surrealist jokes with a bawdy edge, conjuring up images like a Bosch painting. Key phrases echo in obviously horrid laughter the main themes of the play:

> *2nd. Madman.* Hell is a mere glass-house, where the devils are continually blowing up women's souls, on hollow irons, and the fire never goes out.

3rd. Madman. I will lie with every woman in my parish the tenth night: I will tythe them over, like haycocks.

4th. Madman. Shall my pothecary outgo me, because I am a cuckold? I have found out his roguery: he makes alum of his wife's urine, and sells it to puritans that have sore throats with over-straining.

(IV.ii.77–85)

The phrases seem to be random, but stray words stick out vividly as keys to their obsessions—sex, death, hell, religion. They are certainly funny, but the hideous tension of the scene may or may not permit actual laughter. They are men, disguised by madness; Bosola has sworn not to carry on Ferdinand's schemes 'in his own shape', but does so disguised. He appears now as an old man, as though he were interpreter for the masque, and goes on changing roles in a weird fashion. Against him the Duchess finally affirms *her* role:

Duchess. Thou art not mad, sure—dost know me?

Bosola. Yes.

Duchess. Who am I?

Bosola. Thou art a box of worm-seed, at best, but a salvatory of green mummy:—what's this flesh? a little crudded milk, fantastical puff-paste; our bodies are weaker than those paper prisons boys use to keep flies in; more contemptible, since ours is to preserve earthworms. ...

Duchess. Am not I thy Duchess?

Bosola. Thou art some great woman, sure, for riot begins to sit on thy forehead, clad in gray hairs, twenty years sooner than on a merry milkmaid's. ...

Duchess. I am Duchess of Malfi still.   (121–142)

The utterly flat movement of Bosola's prose (in the *De*

Contemptu Mundi tradition) is contrasted with the developing rhythmic power of the Duchess's interjections, even though they are separated more widely than I have space to quote here. The laughter is as effectively silenced here as in *Hamlet*. That final line–'I am Duchess of Malfi still'–is surprising in its brilliant effect, because she has never fulfilled that role before, although she has anticipated it in III.ii. 70–71 (which I quoted) and 137–9:

> Why should only I,
> Of all the other princes of the world,
> Be cas'd up, like a holy relic?

Otherwise she has been the oppressed sister, oppressed woman, and happy housewife. So, out of this sequence of role-playing, 'Duchess' is a role created by very careful art – so memorably, that it impinges as profound truth. The act proceeds through the illusory arts of waxwork and anti-masque into the revelation of this as reality.

Bosola's masquerade continues with yet another role as he changes from tomb-maker to common bellman:

> I am the common bellman
> That usually is sent to condemn'd persons
> The night before they suffer: —

Duchess.   Even now thou said'st
Thou wast a tomb-maker.

Bosola.   'Twas to bring you
By degrees to mortification. Listen:

(IV.ii.173–7)

and he speaks a dirge, the 'straight' version of the Howl the madmen sang before their act and final dance. Cariola protests in an effort to save the Duchess, and provokes another change of key, into pathos (which makes audiences weep):

Cariola. Hence villains, tyrants, murderers! alas!
What will you do with my lady? call for help.

Duchess. To whom? to our next neighbours? they are mad-folks.

Bosola. Remove that noise. ...

Cariola. I will die with her.

Duchess. I pray thee, look thou giv'st my little boy
Some syrup for his cold, and let the girl
Say her prayers, ere she sleep.
[*Executioners force* Cariola *off.*]
Now what you please —
What death?

Bosola. Strangling ... (196–206)

So the end is an impressive stoicism:

Bosola. Yet, methinks, ...
This cord should terrify you?

Duchess. Not a whit:
What would it pleasure me to have my throat cut
With diamonds? or to be smothered
With cassia? or to be shot to death with pearls?
I know death hath ten thousand several doors
For men to take their exits; and 'tis found
They go on such strange geometrical hinges,
You may open them both ways: — any way, for heaven-sake,
So I were out of your whispering ... (213–223)

And so finally:

Pull, and pull strongly, for your able strength
Must pull down heaven upon me ... (230–231)

That death is magnificent, and the variety of responses it demands are superbly controlled. It emerges from the grotesque laughter of madmen, through Bosola's disguised semi-humour, into an affirmation purged of laughter which itself moves on through pathos to the dignified stoicism when control becomes the Duchess's own resistance to her flashes of anger and contempt. But it is constantly revived in act V as Ferdinand's obsessive musings echo its most striking phrases in incoherent parody:

> Strangling is a very quiet death.   (V.iv.34)

> My sister! O! my sister! there's the cause on't:
> *Whether we fall by ambition, blood, or lust*
> *Like diamonds, we are cut with our own dust.*
> (V.v.71–3)

Here, in act IV, the dignity so carefully built up out of its opposite reverts finally to cruel laughter at Cariola's desperate struggle to live:

> *Bosola.*   Delays:—throttle her.

> *Executioner.* She bites, and scratches:—

> *Cariola.*   If you kill me now
> I am damn'd: I have not been at confession
> This two years:—

> *Bosola.*   When?

> *Cariola.*   I am quick with child.

> *Bosola.*   Why then,
> Your credit's sav'd ...   (IV.ii.251–5)

She is abruptly strangled and dragged off stage, where the Duchess still lies. Enter Ferdinand: Bosola protests against his order to murder the children as well, and the weird obsession with wolves, already emerging when he asked the Duchess about her 'cubs', becomes more dominant:

> The death
> Of young wolves is never to be pitied.

> *Bosola.* Fix your eye here:—

> *Ferdinand.*   Constantly. (258–260)

So he does, for the rest of the play:

Cover her face: mine eyes dazzle: she died young.

(264)

The sources of Ferdinand's obsessive insanity are, of course, obscure. They resonate from the beginning, in that strange inflated greatness of the opening - 'Laugh when I laugh' – to the way he is seen as an absolute spectacle – 'The Lord Ferdinand is going to bed', 'The Lord Ferdinand laughs' – as well as in his animal complex, shifting from dormice to wolves. Now, in the deep shock of his sister's death, he looks for explanations: she was his twin, he hoped to inherit her wealth – clues, perhaps, and both had been hinted at before, but they certainly do not 'explain'. Somewhere in the centre of it is certainly the obsession with his sister which is as profoundly sexual as it is possessive, and in its incestuous perversity appallingly sadistic and destructive. Baffled of understanding, he reverts to wolves:

Bosola.   who shall dare
    To reveal this?

Ferdinand.   O, I'll tell thee:
    The wolf shall find her grave, and scrape it up:
    Not to devour the corpse, but to discover
    The horrid murder.

Bosola.   You, not I, shall quake for't.

Ferdinand. Leave me: —   (307–312)

And he finally exits with a superbly vivid image, in total insanity:

    I'll go hunt the badger, by owl-light:
    'Tis a deed of darkness.   (334–5)

That returns us to the ambiguous aura in which one may or may not laugh, but must perceive the laughter in the horror, or vice versa.

Ferdinand may not be fully explicable, but he is psychologically convincing, and his obsessive mind contributes a succession of weird, vivid images of the play. Bosola, perhaps, is not quite convincing. The idea of his sardonic cynical evil gradually yielding to the humanity it perverts—carrying out orders in act IV in disguise and against his conscience and then having the last irony turned against him when he kills Antonio in trying to save him—that *idea* is clear, but in the performance the psychology is not strong enough to sustain it. In particular, the disguises of act IV, as old man, tomb-maker and bellman, are not psychologically clear; they function more effectively as part of the aesthetic structure of the act, the 'art' of the scene, as part of the horrid laughter around the Duchess's death. In other words, psychological insight, though spasmodically fascinating, is only one of the play's multiple perspectives, not its centre. Its positives and negatives play around the central images of life and death which finally move into their last phase with the tragi-farce in act V, set against the last movement of the religious imagery, the insistently beautiful haunting of the echo-scene.

It is by no means universally admitted that the last act does involve serious laughter. Productions of *The Duchess* commonly try to avoid it, in whole or in part, believing, I suppose, that good tragedy is straight tragedy. It is true that there is nothing here so clearly defined as Flamineo's rising from the floor after the mock-suicide, and that therefore laughter seems not to be so clearly channelled as in *The White Devil* (though I have tried to show that it is in act IV). This is partly because Bosola does not sustain the cynical wit which gives Flamineo a consistent tone, like Vindice's; in act V his conscience becomes complete, it is fate, not he, that is the ironist, causing him to kill Antonio when he is trying to save him. The laughter, then, comes from a less specific source and is less easy to define. It rests more pervasively on the ambiguity of tone I have discussed, in which there is no definitive trigger, but a double sense is pervasive, of horror and laughter that are not mutually exclusive; when they laugh and when they don't may vary with different audiences from night to night with the same production. In every performance that I have seen, whether it has been intended or not, there has been laughter before the act was out; but it has varied in quality: when it is clear to an audience that laughter is not intended they – being polite to the actors – hold it in as long as they can, but then when it does come it is inevitably dismissive, a rejection of the play that is being offered them, of the eventually ludicrous solemnity. Where it must come is easily stated, not so easily understood.

By the end of V.v Antonio's body is on stage; the Cardinal, twice stabbed by Bosola and once by Ferdinand, dies too; Ferdinand gives Bosola a death-wound and Bosola kills Ferdinand. Four bodies pile up in a mix-up of accident and intent and some of them die slowly. The fact is that, however handled, an accumulation of bodies builds up towards mirth sooner or later: for some reason one body may be sad, but four is ridiculous. The plays I am discussing all fill the stage with bodies at the end, often (as I said) stylising it as a dance of death: for that is what it is – the plays are ultimately *about* death, and they make a spectacle of it, whether stylised or not. Shakespeare rarely has more than one or two deaths; the obvious exception is *Hamlet*, where the confused piling up of Gertrude, Laertes, Claudius and finally Hamlet himself does frequently provoke laughter, which is very effectively silenced by Hamlet's dying words, Horatio's epitaph, and Fortinbras's. In act IV, as I have shown, Webster uses a similar technique; but the last words of act V are neutral and formal, not powerfully moving, so Webster here does not exercise that restraint, but leaves the laughter in place as part of the play's conclusion.

But the laughter is certainly not merely random: it does have a number of cues which solemn productions sometimes cut – and are rewarded for their pains by getting the laughs anyhow. V.i is a brief, almost choric, scene for Antonio, Delio and Pescara, distancing the horrors of act IV with new action, life seemingly going on

with figures who will sustain it. V.ii opens with the doctor
ludicrously confident of curing Ferdinand's madness. His
long speech expounding Lycanthropy in what are, in fact,
standard text-book terms, is usually laughed at, perhaps
because of its prosy tediousness, and his attempt to frighten
Ferdinand into sanity is always funny, because of its absurd
failure:

> *Pescara.* Doctor, he did not fear you throughly.

> *Doctor.* True, I was somewhat too forward.
>
> (V.ii.83-4)

Ferdinand's madness is thus given a comic context; it is in
itself potentially funny, but powerfully so – he is a wolf,
not the tame dormouse the doctor would make of him.
They leave the Cardinal and Bosola alone to conspire, but
conspiracy itself is becoming a dry absurdity: Bosola is
deceiving the Cardinal, he will execute no further plots.
To them, enter Julia, the Cardinal's mistress:

> Sir, will you come in to supper?

> *Cardinal.*   I am busy, leave me.

> *Julia.* [*Aside*] What an excellent shape hath that fellow!
>
> *Exit.* (121-2)

The Cardinal leaves, Julia re-enters, and uses two pistols to
seduce Bosola in what becomes a comic parody of the
Duchess seducing Antonio four acts earlier:

> I am sudden with you;
> We that are great women of pleasure use to cut off
> These uncertain wishes, and unquiet longings,
> And in an instant join the sweet delight
> And the pretty excuse together ...   (192-6)

Julia is a 'great woman-of-pleasure', meaning a courtesan;
the Duchess was a great woman, bent on pleasure; but
their language is neatly similar. So this is a second comic
scene, very different in tone from the first: this is what is

usually known as comedy of manners, in high society. It seems to be entirely light in more than one sense, comic relief perhaps, but on the Cardinal's return it transposes abruptly into Julia's death. The Cardinal swears her to secrecy as he confesses procuring the Duchess's murder:

Julia.   O heaven! sir, what have you done?

Cardinal. How now? how settles this? think you your
                                                    bosom
   Will be a grave, dark and obscure enough,
   For such a secret?

Julia.   You have undone yourself, sir.

Cardinal. Why?

Julia.   It lies not in me to conceal it. (270–274)

He assumes because she is being honest about her lightness; actually it is because she knows that Bosola, hidden for her pleasure, can overhear (and there is the further irony that that doesn't matter, since he carried out the murder):

Cardinal.   No?
   Come, I will swear you to't upon this book.

Julia. Most religiously.

Cardinal.   Kiss it. (274–6)

The book, of course, is poisoned. Julia dies quickly, and with an echo of Flamineo's dignity:

Bosola. O foolish woman,
   Couldst not thou have poison'd him?

Julia.   'Tis weakness,
   Too much to think what should have been done—I
                                                    go,
   I know not whither.   [*Dies.*]   (286–9)

Julia is witty, slight, and briefly moving. The Cardinal, wearily carrying on his obsessive (but now meaningless)

conspiracy and murder, becomes grotesquely ludicrous. He
is sane, but haunted by guilt. Ferdinand is insane,
powerfully manic. Bosola's handling is savagely jokey.

V.iii is totally different, the consciously beautiful echo
scene, when Antonio hears his dead Duchess's voice in the
echo and eventually sees her as a vision. Her image is so
powerfully linked to potential life that she seems almost set
up for resurrection: long after her first death, after her
brother's staring at her beauty, she startled Bosola by a
brief revival; now the illusory echo brings her vividly to
Antonio's eyes. V.iv returns to the Cardinal, carefully
organising the attendant lords to ignore any noises they
may hear in the night (he plans to bury Julia then). In the
confusion, Bosola kills Antonio, imagining him to be the
Cardinal. Then in V.v the Cardinal at last reveals the depth
of his guilty agony in a strange and powerful soliloquy:

> I am puzzled in a question about hell:
> He says, in hell there's one material fire,
> And yet it shall not burn all men alike.
> Lay him by:—how tedious is a guilty conscience!
> When I look into the fish-ponds, in my garden,
> Methinks I see a thing, arm'd with a rake
> That seems to strike at me ...   (V.v.1–7)

Bosola enters with Antonio's body, and reveals his intent
to kill the Cardinal. The Cardinal cries out, of course, and
the lords appear on the upper stage, joking about the
performance he had told them they would hear:

Malateste.   Listen:—

Cardinal. My dukedom for rescue!

Roderigo.   Fie upon his counterfeiting!

Malateste. Why, 'tis not the cardinal.

Roderigo.   Yes, yes, 'tis he:
  But I'll see him hang'd, ere I'll go down to him.

Cardinal. Here's a plot upon me, I am assaulted! I am lost,

    Unless some rescue!

Grisolan.   He doth this pretty well:

    But it will not serve to laugh me out of mine honour.

Cardinal. The sword's at my throat: —

Roderigo.   You would not bawl so loud then.

Malateste. Come, come:

    Let's go to bed: he told us thus much aforehand.

                                         (19–28)

Their foppish humour marks the laughter here: but it is also grotesque. All these grotesque figures moving in the dark, executing plots which misfire, and dying by mistake: it is grotesquely ludicrous, horribly funny. And when all are dead or dying, the same group of affected lords enters on the main stage to release our final laughter:

Pescara. How now, my lord?

Malateste.   O, sad disaster!

Roderigo.   How comes this?   (80)

He might well ask: the question (when it is not cut) brings the house down. To cut that entry (which is often done) is to castrate the play by trying to suppress the laughter which needs its definitive release–and which, as I said, will come in any case.

The cues for laughter are, then, elaborately placed throughout the act, and their relevance should be clear. Not all are of the same kind, and with some of them the quality would be very different, almost light, if they were not juxtaposed with the brilliantly moving passages which are generally well-known: Julia's curt stoicism, the Cardinal's heavy guilt, Ferdinand's obscurely pertinent savagery, Bosola's desperate irony – those give the act its weight, and make the countertone a necessarily, and intelligibly, *horrid* laughter. Allowed its place, the laughter is by no means a rejection of the play, but an integral part of it; once its main placing is assured we may elsewhere laugh or not as we please, for both the horror and the laughter are its attitude to the lives and deaths the play presents.

The discrimination of different kinds of comedy, as well as the radical contrast of the echo scene, indicate the more deliberate and controlled range of the play when it is compared with *The White Devil*. It is one of Webster's most distinctive achievements, to find the appropriate dramatic forms for that range, and therefore the appropriate languages; it makes for the divergence of different modes within his play which is often seen as inconsistency, so it is important to recognise that inconsistency in this sense is a positive principle in the play. The most helpful discussion of this is by Inga-Stina Ewbank, expounding the idea of 'perspective' (2). In modern use the word has been confined to the optical illusion of depth created by parallel lines that, in the drawing, are moving towards a point; in the sixteenth and seventeenth century it was more widely applied to illusion in visual art, but particularly to a favourite device of mannerist art in which a picture seen as one image from one angle becomes quite another when you move to a different position. The best known example, though dozens were produced (often as play-things), is Holbein's *The Ambassadors*: seemingly a portrait study of two prosperous men, it has a large indecipherable object in the centre low down which, when viewed from the side, becomes a skull and so radically alters the composition of the painting and its implication. The transformation relies so obviously on ingenuity that it appears to be a mere trick, yet it is clear how aptly the concealed skull comments on the confident images of human pride. That, in the forms of dramatic illusion, seems to be the idea behind Webster's apparent discontinuities in both plays, but it is far more fully developed in *The Duchess of Malfi* than in *The White Devil*, and accounts for its larger range.

The White Devil seems to be largely about death, and the processes through which men and women rush towards death; so does *The Duchess*, but the later play also offers far clearer and more varied prospects of the possibilities of life. Vittoria, indeed, is a vitally interesting person alive, but her life has no recognisable context in which it might flourish, unless that of a great courtesan which she rejects; the result is that she seems to be committed to self-perfection only in death. The Duchess too reaches final definition in death, when she is more strictly splendid than ever before, and she too is denied a context for her living beauty. But she is *denied* it; what it would be, in her domestic happiness, is clearly established. Vittoria's marriage to the condemned greatness is never suggested as such a prospect at all. The Cardinal and Ferdinand are, like Bracciano and Francisco, the evil of preposterous grandeur, but again in the later play the distortion of normal psyches which 'greatness' generates is much more clearly established, so that even there an idea of normal life has its positive force. Lastly, as I have said, Bosola's discovery of his conscience is a far more extended matter than Flamineo's, and it partly dictates the different form of the end of the play. These differences are important, but it would be wrong to leave the stress there, and more wrong still if I seem to sentimentalise *The Duchess of Malfi*; its structure seems to me an extension of that of *The White Devil*, permitting an additional dimension in the perspective, not a radical change: the logic of definition in death, of horrid laughter at death-in-life, is the vital centre of both plays.

V

The Changeling

It is characteristic of Jacobean drama that a great deal of it was the result, like broadcasting scripts today, of collaboration. It is a romantic prejudice which assumes the superiority of single authorship, and the labours of scholarship which have gone into trying to distinguish individual contributions are largely wasted. It is usual to assign the 'main plot' to Middleton and the 'sub-plot' to Rowley, but the stylistic tests adduced can only really demonstrate the difference of language between tragedy and comedy, which any single author, especially one brought up on Elizabethan linguistic theories, would make. It is, however, a fact that the play is unusually sharply divided between its tragic and comic modes although the theme—roughly, women and sex—is common to both. In the main plot, Beatrice-Joanna is betrothed to Alonso de Piracquo, falls in love with Alsemero, becomes totally involved with De Flores who finally kills her and himself. In the sub-plot Isabella is married to the jealous doctor Alibius who runs a quack asylum, she is courted by Antonio (pretending idiocy) and Francisco (pretending madness), flirts with both, but finally hands them over and is reconciled to her husband.

If the theme is the same, the handling of the two plots is radically different. The Isabella story is light, witty, very

bawdy. It *touches* violence, cruelty, sadism, social in-
difference to mental disease, etcetera, but it touches them
lightly and never quite takes them seriously enough to
allow them to become seriously disturbing, so it can
emerge into song, dance and a happy ending. The
Beatrice-Joanna story, on the other hand, is sharp, moral,
high-flown, very perceptive, obscene, horrible, and committed to ultimate disaster. It explores sexual experience
through devious routes to a terrifying conclusion. The
events of the two plots are brought briefly together at the
end, but their tones can seemingly never meet; yet not
only theme, but incident, behaviour and so on are
constantly echoing each other. Even Beatrice-Joanna's
noble husband turns out to be an amateur scientist
(where Alibius is an acknowledged, if not qualified,
doctor), and uses chemical tests for his wife's virginity.

I have expressed the contrast in genre terms, tragedy and
comedy; there is equally a social contrast. Beatrice-Joanna
inhabits an aristocratic world, and her values are aristocratic: moral concepts of good and evil are absolute, and
Honour is supreme, destroyed by a no less absolute Love.
Isabella is middle class, shrewd, mercantile; her values are
sensible, flexible; her husband's jealousy is ridiculous and
merits cuckolding; she isn't much bothered by scruples, but
she is by danger, and therefore she discreetly withdraws.
So the social contrast implies a moral contrast. The main
plot depends on the moral cited in *Women Beware
Women*–'Beware of off'ring the first-fruits to sin'–
whereas in the sub-plot there are no first-fruits, since
Isabella is not a virgin, and the sin she contemplates does
not appear as a very great one in any case. It is difficult to
grasp how two things so seemingly different in aesthetic,
social, moral standards can co-habit in a single play. Both
have equal claims to the abused term 'realistic', in quite
different ways. The art of the theatre may imitate life, but
in its own terms, and this play explores those terms to
yield an image of experience more complex than either
genre (comedy or tragedy) can readily yield alone. The

complexity which has become familiar in other plays is here more sharply distinguished into a form that is more like two-plays-in-one.

The play owes, I think, a great deal to Shakespeare's *Romeo and Juliet,* though the similarities are hardly obvious. Shakespeare's play is set as a tragedy, but for two acts uses the conventions and the languages which he has elsewhere developed for comedy; and it is through a comic figure, Mercutio, that it shifts to death (1); yet it retains a strong comic element even into the final scene. It is comedy-and-tragedy, but it is nowhere near farce. It is also, like *The Changeling,* set in a small city-state, where aristocracy and bourgeoisie are necessarily closely intertwined, but which nevertheless leaves the heroine in a narrowly exclusive world. The demarcation is simplified in Middleton's play, where Beatrice-Joanna's father appears to be the head of the local hierarchy, which Juliet's was not; and Juliet's world has more inhabitants than Beatrice-Joanna's which seems to be almost as small as Prospero's and Miranda's in *The Tempest.* The likeness and difference is most obvious in the heroines: both seem to be experiencing sexual responses to men for the first time; but with Juliet this is entirely a matter of her age, whereas for Beatrice-Joanna it is apparently because she has never encountered men (or at least eligible men) outside her father's household before, and she reacts to them much like Miranda:

> O brave new world
> That has such people in't!   (*Tempest* V.i.183–4)

For Juliet, on the other hand, it is a first sexual awakening in a pubescent girl who sees men enough, but suddenly sees Romeo as she has never seen before. Miranda is amazed by the new men, but she does not see them as more beautiful than Ferdinand; Beatrice-Joanna sees each new man as he appears as more lovely than the last, and in that she is more like Romeo, though much less light-hearted.

Beatrice-Joanna is no doubt young, but her actual age is

not given, and there is no such stress on her being
extremely young as there is with Juliet; her ignorance
emerges largely from not seeing, from the deprivation of
social isolation. The only man she knows she reacts to
physically, very violently:

> *De Flores.* Lady, your father —
>
> *Beatrice.*   Is in health, I hope.
>
> *De Flores.* Your eye shall instantly instruct you, lady.
>   He's coming hitherward.
>
> *Beatrice.*   What needed then
>   Your duteous preface? I had rather
>   He had come unexpected; you must stall
>   A good presence with unnecessary blabbing:
>   And how welcome for your part you are,
>   I'm sure you know.
>
> *De Flores.* [*aside.*]   Will't never mend this scorn
>   One side nor other?...   Well,
>   Fates do your worst, I'll please myself with sight
>   Of her, at all opportunities,
>   If but to spite her anger ...
>
>   (I.i.93–105)

The stress on 'sight' is conspicuously sustained through
what follows, Beatrice-Joanna's first meeting with Alsemero: within 100 lines the sight of him has reoriented her
responses:

> I shall change my saint, I fear me, I find
> A giddy turning in me ...   (155–6)

It seems that her betrothed had so struck her sight before
(it was by no means a marriage imposed by her father);
now it is Alsemero. No other sense has yet been involved:
at the end of the scene it is again De Flores who offers
touch:

> *Vermandero.*   Look, girl, thy glove's fall'n;
>   Stay, stay, — De Flores, help a little.   [*Exeunt others.*]

De Flores.   Here, lady.
                                        [*Offers the glove.*]

Beatrice. Mischief on your officious forwardness!
    Who bade you stoop? They touch my hand no more:
    There, for t'other's sake I part with this,
            [*Takes off the other glove and throws it down.*]
    Take 'em and draw thine own skin off with 'em.
                                                    Exit.

De Flores. Here's a favour come, with a mischief! Now I
                                                    know
    She had rather wear my pelt tann'd in a pair
    Of dancing pumps, than I should thrust my fingers
    Into her sockets here, I know she hates me,
    Yet cannot choose but love her ...   (225–235)

The hint of physical contact produces violent language in
both of them. Beatrice-Joanna is continually made more
aware of De Flores than of anyone else, and her revulsion
from him is more immediately felt, and of longer standing,
than her attraction to anyone else. Her behaviour is, in
fact, a kind of innocence, but a very peculiar kind; and,
being innocence, it is something of which she has no
understanding at all.

    Hence, by II.ii, Beatrice-Joanna has changed partners as
easily as Romeo – but in a very different tone. She declares
her feeling for Alsemero:

    I have within mine eye all my desires;

                                                    (II.ii.8)

and proceeds to organise the situation with unhesitating
directness; not by Juliet's sexual candour, but by an instant
decision to have Alonso murdered, and murdered by, of
course, De Flores. Their encounter is a masterpiece of
limited vision. De Flores has watched Beatrice-Joanna with
Alsemero:

    I have watch'd this meeting, and do wonder much
    What shall become of t'other; I'm sure both

Cannot be serv'd unless she transgress; happily
Then I'll put in for one: for if a woman
Fly from one point, from him she makes a husband,
She spreads and mounts then like arithmetic,
One, ten, a hundred, a thousand, ten thousand,
Proves in time sutler to an army royal.
Now do I look to be most richly rail'd at,
Yet I must see her.   (57–66)

He so far believes himself as to assume that Beatrice turned whore will readily sleep with him. She has another thought:

Why, put case I loath'd him
As much as youth and beauty hates a sepulchre,
Must I needs show it? Cannot I keep that secret,
And serve my turn upon him?   (66–9)

To 'serve her turn' has another meaning than what she intends: all the language of the scene tends towards unconscious *double entendre* – but what *is* intended has the same direction. Beatrice-Joanna, to hire De Flores as murderer, pretends to make love to him, and he is partly deceived:

'Tis half an act of pleasure
To hear her talk thus to me.

Beatrice-Joanna.   When w'are us'd
To a hard face, 'tis not so unpleasing;
It mends still in opinion, hourly mends,
I see it by experience.

De Flores. [aside.]   I was blest
To light upon this minute; I'll make use on't. (86–91)

He will, but not so easily as he supposes:

Beatrice.   Would creation —

De Flores. Ay, well said, that's it.

Beatrice.   Had form'd me man.

De Flores. Nay, that's not it.

Beatrice.   Oh, 'tis the soul of freedom!
  I should not then be forc'd to marry one
  I hate beyond all depths, I should have power
  Then to oppose my loathings, nay, remove 'em
  For ever from my sight.   (107–113)

She means, of course, Alonso, but the words apply to De
Flores. The result is a perfect misunderstanding: he assumes
that she will sleep with him, she that she can hire him:

        [*gives him money*]—there's to encourage thee:
      As thou art forward and thy service dangerous,
      Thy reward shall be precious.

(much of the scene depends on repeated play on the word
'service')

De Flores.   That I have thought on;
  I have assur'd myself of that beforehand,
  And know it will be precious, the thought ravishes.
                                       (128–132)

She does not respond to his suggestion – she cannot, for she
has not the slightest idea what he means; on the other hand
he takes her to be playing out a more total hypocrisy than
she is. And so, as he deceives her, he is himself deceived:

Beatrice.   When the deed's done,
  I'll furnish thee with all things for thy flight;
  Thou may'st live bravely in another country.

De Flores. Ay, ay, we'll talk of that hereafter.

Beatrice. [*aside.*]   I shall rid myself
  Of two inveterate loathings at one time,
  Piracquo, and his dog-face.   *Exit.*

De Flores.   Oh my blood!
  Methinks I feel her in my arms already,
  Her wanton fingers combing out this beard,
  And being pleased, praising this bad face. (141–9)

So he conducts Alonso through the dark passages of the castle and kills him in the cellars.

The trap springs when he and Beatrice next meet. She offers money, and he is contemptuous; she has no idea what he is after, he is incredulous that she does not understand. When at last she does understand she is morally indignant:

> Why, 'tis impossible thou canst be so wicked,
> Or shelter such a cunning cruelty,
> To make his death the murderer of my honour!
> Thy language is so bold and vicious,
> I cannot see which way I can forgive it
> With any modesty.
>
> *De Flores.*   Push, you forget yourself!
>   A woman dipp'd in blood, and talk of modesty?
> (III.iv.120–126)

And so:

> Y'are the deed's creature; by that name
> You lost your first condition, and I challenge you,
> As peace and innocency has turn'd you out,
> And made you one with me.   (137–140)

Her 'innocency' is perfectly caught, and there is an inverted innocence too in the difficulty he has in grasping how her mind goes.

She becomes more deeply caught than that. The murder was arranged so that she could marry Alsemero, whose highest value and constant theme is his honour. His notion of getting rid of Alonso was to fight a duel, risking his own life, and that she instantly forbade. Honour demands the cult of virginity: to be his wife she must go virgin to the marriage bed. And once she has yielded to De Flores she is deflowered. Worse, she has been noticed talking secretly with De Flores and their complicity is rumoured. Alsemero is an amateur scientist, and he plans to apply chemical tests for her virginity. She can cope with that by discovering and mimicking their effects, but she cannot face the first night in bed, and so sends her truly virginal but very willing maid into him in the dark. That makes another party to her crimes, and so another murder. The form that takes is intensified by the maid's uninhibited delight in bed: she long overstays her time, and to force her out De Flores and Beatrice have to stage a fire and burn Diaphanta in it. So their complicity carries itself on:

> *Beatrice.*   I'm forc'd to love thee now,
> 'Cause thou provid'st so carefully for my honour.
>
> *De Flores.* 'Slid , it concerns the safety of us both,
> Our pleasure and continuance.
>
> (V.i.47–50)

It has come to that: the pleasure has become as mutual as the dependence; she has been forced to love him, and she does:

> His face loathes one,
> But look upon his care, who would not love him?
> The east is not more beauteous than his service.
>
> (70–72)

The loathing and the caste-feeling transpose into their opposites in a last pun on 'service', without which the allusion to the exotic east would have no meaning. So, discovered, they finally die together. When Beatrice-Joanna tells Alsemero that she has not dishonoured his bed, it is true in the tricksy sense that she has never entered it. But 'honour' is a word that has been put through all its paces, and there *is* a final honour in the self-knowledge which Beatrice-Joanna can ultimately express to her father:

> Oh come not near me, sir, I shall defile you:
> I am that of your blood was taken from you
> For your better health ...
>
> (V.iii.149–151)

And De Flores, too, answering Alsemero:

> Yes; and the while I coupled with your mate
> At barley-brake; now we are left in hell. (162–3)

They go to hell together, more perfect in their corruption than the dubiously honourable figures they leave behind. The perfection of it, its total inversion of the images of Love and Honour, is of course essential to its tragic force, and it is a remarkable artistic achievement. It is worked out through a startling psychological insight, and a dramatic and linguistic subtlety rare even in Jacobean drama. Once Beatrice has given her first-fruits to sin, the rest follows with inescapable dramatic logic. But that very perfection raises problems. Middleton is commonly praised for his 'realism', but moral perfection of this kind belongs to art and not to any other accessible reality. Yet the psychological realism with which the plot is handled is peculiarly convincing; without that it would be meaningless. Given that our attention is so brilliantly drawn to that, we are bound to perceive that any person who carries such moral logic to its conclusion is, strictly, not normal; at the least, abnormally obsessive – in short, mad. Take De Flores and Beatrice-Joanna out of the play into a law-court and it is immediately a question if they are fit to plead, they are so manifestly insane. But Beatrice's madness is built on a strange obsession, a total assumption of the twin values of her aristocratic world: Honour, and Love. Her story loses all meaning if those two are not accepted as absolute values, and it is precisely from those absolute values that the tragedy derives its splendour. The central figures never question them; Alsemero, Vermandero, the Piracquo brothers, Beatrice-Joanna herself, all take them for granted as distinguishing their world. Beatrice manipulates them, she does not question them; and if De Flores does, that is precisely why he is so clearly known to be a villain. And yet in his own perverse way he is moulded by them: it is as essential to him as to Alsemero to have Beatrice's virginity:

> For I place wealth after the heels of pleasure,
> And were I not resolv'd in my belief
> That thy virginity were perfect in thee,
> I should but take my recompense with grudging,
> As if I had but half my hopes I agreed for.
>
> (III.iv.115–19)

De Flores is a poor gentleman, and his mores are created by his caste as well as by his poverty. He is forced to live by his wits, so that his wits are sharp, like Vindice's, Flamineo's and Bosola's. His wit continually exposes the absurdity of the moral pretension, and therefore of the artistic perfection, right to the end of the play:

> *Alsemero.* What's this blood upon your band, De Flores?
>
> *De Flores.* Blood? No, sure, 'twas wash'd since.
>
> *Alsemero.*   Since when, man?
>
> *De Flores.* Since t'other day I got a knock
> In a sword and dagger school; I think 'tis out.
>
> *Alsemero.* Yes, 'tis almost out, but 'tis perceiv'd, though.
> I had forgot my message; this it is:
> What price goes murder?
>
> *De Flores.*   How, sir?
>
> *Alsemero.*   I ask you, sir;
> My wife's behindhand with you, she tells me,
> For a brave bloody blow you gave for her sake
> Upon Piracquo.
>
> *De Flores.*   Upon? 'Twas quite through him, sure ...
>
> (V.iii.95–104)

Finally, the boasting that is, as with Vindice, a corollary of his wit, emerges in explanation of his murder:

> Yes, and her honour's prize
> Was my reward; I thank life for nothing
> But that pleasure: it was so sweet to me
> That I have drunk up all, left none behind
> For any man to pledge me.

Vermandero. Horrid villain! (167–171)

Horrid, certainly; and funny with it.

To criticise the main plot, then, you have to stand back from its basic postulates, heroic honour and heroic love. The realism for which Middleton is celebrated depends on them, and they are not realistic at all. But to arrive at this comment is not to get outside this play at all; its other half, the comic plot of Isabella, her doctor husband and his madhouse, says all that: all the characters are fools and madmen. It functions in that sense as an immediate parody of the main plot, and by contrast with that, it seems to have no values at all. The only distinction between the inhabitants of Alibius's asylum is that the Fools are harmless and the Madmen are dangerous. The sane men, the doctor and his servant Lollio, care only for the cash value, the profit to be made from looking after the embarrassing lunatics of rich families: the cash paid down for board and lodging, and the additional cash that can be made by exhibiting them in public. It is possible – because the comic scenes, for most of the play, are entirely separate from the main plot – to regard them as a trivial irrelevance, but they are nothing of the kind. The relationship is most pointedly exploited in act III: De Flores leads Alonso through the dark regions of the fortress and kills him in the back passage, then exits with the body. Then

> *Enter* Isabella *and* Lollio.
> *Isabella.* Why, sirrah? Whence have you commission
>   To fetter the doors against me?
>   If you keep me in a cage, pray whistle to me,
>   Let me be doing something.
>
> (III.iii.1–4)

The prison, fetters, cage are the locks of her husband's house; but they inherit the images of the fortress from the previous scene. The preoccupations of the fools and madmen, and of Alibius and Lollio, are the same as their betters':

> Is it your master's pleasure, or your own,
> To keep me in this pinfold?
>
> *Lollio.* 'Tis for my master's pleasure, lest being taken in another man's corn, you might be pounded in another place.
>
> *Isabella.* 'Tis very well, and he'll prove very wise. (7–11)

That enables the reference of the whole sub-plot to be made explicit:

> *Lollio.* He says you have company enough in the house, if you please to be sociable, of all sorts of people.
>
> *Isabella.* Of all sorts? Why, here's none but fools and madmen.
>
> *Lollio.* Very well: and where will you find any other, if you should go abroad? There's my master and I to boot too.
>
> *Isabella.* Of either sort one, a madman and a fool.
> (12–17)

Beatrice-Joanna lives in a literal fortress – all Vermandero's guests are shown the defences – and vice versa, her world too is all fools and madmen, and she too has no larger choice than a madman and a fool, De Flores and Vermandero.

What follows first parodies what has earlier gone on between Beatrice-Joanna and De Flores. Isabella is left alone with the fool Tony, and she starts an affair with him. Tony is in fact a gentleman in disguise and not a literal half-wit: in the tragic plot people are not what they seem, in the comic plot this is represented by actual disguise.

Lollio sees them kissing and tries to turn his knowledge to advantage:

> Come, sweet rogue; kiss me, my little Lacedemonian.
> Let me feel how thy pulses beat; thou hast a thing
> about thee would do a man pleasure, I'll lay my hand
> on't. (234–7)

The madmen offstage have cried out as part of their game of barley-brake, 'Catch there, catch the last couple in hell!' (165), which De Flores will echo at the end of the play. By this point the scene has moved from parody of what has already happened between De Flores and Beatrice, into what will happen in III.iv immediately afterwards: this scene follows the murder of Alonso, and precedes De Flores demanding Beatrice's virginity.

The two plots mirror each other, but not exactly. Isabella's chastity is at stake, but not her virginity, for she has no such thing. What she might have to lose is no absolute value, and (in a light and bawdy comedy) doesn't in itself matter very much at all–except that it matters to her who she sleeps with, and it won't be Lollio because she doesn't want him and is far too shrewd to be trapped or cajoled into having him. We are here in a very different world from the tragic one; one that is much more obviously corrupt, and yet in truth much less so. A world of madmen where people are reassuringly sane. The two plots are very intricately interrelated, but not by simple parallels. Lollio is not the only one who can echo De Flores: Tony, the changeling, the gentleman disguised as fool, can do it too, and verbally more closely:

> Look you but cheerfully, and in your eyes
> I shall behold mine own deformity,
> And dress myself up fairer; I know this shape
> Becomes me not, but in those bright mirrors
> I shall array me handsomely. (185–9)

The perspectives in which the plots bear on each other shift continually; they must, or the play would become a simple thesis instead of the interaction of alternative worlds. In the other direction, the questions which the sub-plot so pertinently asks about the absolute values of the main plot are also asked within that itself, and in ways which relate it to the comedy. Beatrice-Joanna, to avoid discovery, has to pretend extreme fear of sexual initiation in order to persuade her maid to take her place in bed. It is an act, but it is acting the role she would in any case have expected to play: the cult of virginity (as essential to De Flores as to Alsemero) demanded it of her. But, conscious of playing it, she overplays, and to Diaphanta such a feeling is merely incredible (as it is to Emilia in *Othello*). She is, as Beatrice is not, still a virgin, and she, too, has a lover coming, Alsemero's companion Jasperino; but she is longing for pleasure and is not at all preserving her virginity for him: she leaps at the chance to lie with Alsemero and enjoys it so totally she long overstays her time:

Beatrice. Oh, y'are a jewel!

Diaphanta.   Pardon frailty, madam;
    In troth I was so well, I ev'n forgot myself.

                                                    (V.i.77–8)

For that she dies horribly, and De Flores grotesquely points the moral:

                                        Oh poor virginity!
        Thou hast paid dearly for't.   (104–5)

But there is no moral to that event, it is simply the vile conclusion to a delightful paganism and any attempt to moralise would be disgusting. So the whole moral insistence of the tragedy is threatened by the amoral vitality of Diaphanta's life and death. Although there was not a necessary social distinction in the seventeenth century of lady's maid from her mistress, that is clearly used here to illuminate the aristocratic obsession with their moral cults.

Comedy and Tragedy then bear very closely on each other, but yet remain self-sufficient and complete, and in that sense free of each other. That is why they have often been mistaken as irrelevant to each other. It is necessary that they should have the independence as well as the dependence: I have discussed the artistic completeness of tragedy, and the same point has to be made about the comedy. It too is complete in its own terms, and its very different realism is equally limited by that completeness. Comedy is certainly not 'perfect', but it is excellent. The terms, here, are very funny, bawdy, and in their own way not less moral: Isabella sleeps with none of her lovers, and her husband's eyes are opened to the folly of his jealousy, so they survive and can hope to go on doing so. Not impressively, not with any splendour, but both practically and probably. In that, unlike the tragedy, it is realistic. But it too depends on particular values, or the lack of them: roughly, cash and convenience – and nothing more disturbing than that. It, too, is therefore acutely realistic, and yet unrealistic: for no one is so conveniently shrewd, nor so comfortably free of more extreme emotions. Comedy constructs out of its sharp observation of common life a world of art as selective and exclusive as that of tragedy.

That, then, makes the entire play: a comedy and a tragedy, at once separate and very intricately interlocked. They are related to each other in much the same way as anti-masque was to masque, and are actually linked by traditional allegorical motifs: the Castle and the House are derived from their medieval and renaissance significance as emblems of both the world and the human body. The peculiar imaginative power of De Flores' leading Alonso through the dark passages is that the suggestive language long established for him is sustained there: it is also a journey through the organs of a female body to an anal death, *and* a descent into hell. The play can make use of allegorical allusion, but it is not in the least an allegory. Its theme is human sexuality and human values; they appear in tragedy just as much as in comedy, but in a very different form. Alibius and Alsemero are both doctors, but Alibius turns his profession into money, whereas Alsemero tries to provide a scientific justification for his value-system. The tests for virginity are every bit as absurd and as funny as Alibius' cuckoldry, but they are no more absurd than the construction of a tragedy on such a cult. If virginity is a physical reality it should at least be demonstrable; but absolute honour and absolute love require an absolute virginity, which can't be shown.

So the moral implications of tragedy and comedy stand in contradistinction; not in perfect opposition, nothing so simple, but seeming to represent irreconcileable worlds. Either alone would seem to offer a conclusion; juxtaposed together they cannot. But they do not therefore cancel each other out, nor can this be reduced to a matter of 'raising all the questions': both forms do, ultimately, make statements, but different ones. Their coexistence in such definitive form is, even by Jacobean standards, unusual, and it has become unfamiliar through later centuries although much recent drama tends towards the same perception. It tends to make us feel that our mental eyes are crossed, for it renders impossible any summary statement of what we see; but outside the theatre we are accustomed to our own ambivalence, and although it is difficult to state the simultaneous effect it is by no means difficult to experience it–any more than it is difficult to laugh and to weep at the same events.

It does, however, require, and make possible, a further discrimination about the forms of laughter. The comedy is, in Bergson's sense, normative: it uses laughter as a corrective agent, which even inside the play brings Alibius to see 'reason', and presumably encourages the audience to avoid irrational jealousy. But the laughter in the tragedy is of quite another kind: De Flores needs evidence of Alonso's death, the ring won't come off his finger so he cuts off finger and all and gives it to Beatrice as a particularly obscene symbol:

I've a token for you.

Beatrice. For me?

De Flores.   But it was sent somewhat unwillingly,
   I could not get the ring without the finger.

Beatrice. Bless me! What hast thou done?

De Flores.   Why, is that more
   Than killing the whole man? ...

Beatrice. 'Tis the first token my father made me send
                                          him.

De Flores. And I made him send it back again
   For his last token; I was loath to leave it,
   And I'm sure dead men have no use of jewels. ...

Beatrice. I pray, bury the finger, but the stone
   You may make use on shortly; the true value,
   Take't of my truth, is near three hundred ducats.

De Flores. 'Twill hardly buy a capcase for one's
                              conscience, though,
   To keep it from the worm, as fine as 'tis.

                                    (III.iv.26–45)

The moral and imaginative shock is close to Tourneur and
Webster, the savage laughter of the main plot is made
explicit in De Flores' ironies. The virginity tests are
certainly funny, rather in the manner of the doctor's
dealings with lycanthropy in *The Duchess*, and laughter at
them is apt, but scarcely savage enough to play a full part:
it seems more like part of the sub-plot wandered into the
main. So does Diaphanta's pagan pleasure, but there the
reversal becomes fully savage in her callous and mocking
extermination, a *joke* that is a distorted image of hell-fire as
punishment for her delight in life. As the madmen called
out in their game:

   Catch there, catch the last couple in hell!

and De Flores echoed them at the end:

> Yes; and the while I coupled with your mate
> At barley-brake; now we are left in hell.

Laughter and hell-fire are united in folk-game: the resonant allusion suggests an ultimate stylisation in terms of game-playing. Here it is left at suggestion, but in *Women Beware Women* a chess game symbolises the central seduction, and the play moves progressively from domestic naturalism to a final fantastic banquet and masque.

VI

Women Beware Women

There is no evidence at all for dating either of Middleton's tragedies, so we cannot know which was written first. I am discussing them in the order in which I think of them, but nothing I say should be read as depending on that sequence. The plays are, in any case, fairly closely related, whether they were written close in time to each other or not, and the priority of either would be intelligible. Both heroines, Bianca and Beatrice-Joanna, are unusually young (Bianca is said to be 'about sixteen', by the messenger at III.ii.99), and with them both, tragedy partly derives from their inexperience, the readiness with which their passions alter, and the facile clumsiness of their moves into crime (Beatrice-Joanna employing De Flores, Bianca setting up an unscheduled masque which goes wrong, for a murder motivated more by pique than by necessity). Neither of them is given the extreme youth of Juliet, but the psychology of inexperience is made more explicit for Beatrice. Both plays, too, depend on relating two distinct social environments: the well-to-do citizen's – Dr. Alibius's household and Leantio the factor's – with the ducal court of a small city state. In *Women Beware Women* there is an intermediate household round which the play pivots, Livia's. She can treat Leantio's widowed mother as a neighbour-gossip yet also entertain the duke to dinner when, admittedly, he is bent on fornication; but he is not obliged to be incognito in this environment. In each of these points *The Changeling* is more explicit, while the grafting together of the separate strands in *Women Beware Women* can be held to be the more elegant solution. Both plays are remarkable for their structural ingenuity, and for the highly ambivalent identification of moral/tragic/aesthetic 'glory' with social elevation.

Women Beware Women opens with apparent naturalism in a carefully defined humble factor's home, and develops by deliberate stages towards extreme stylization of the court masque in act V, in which almost all the principals are killed by one another. The remarkable control this calls for distinguishes Middleton from the earlier dramatists: Tourneur's play, I argued, has in fact a firm structure but it is hardly conspicuous in performance; in his play, and still in Webster's, wild chaos is more immediately apparent than structural order. With Middleton, especially with *Women Beware Women*, that situation is reversed: chaotic experience is still the subject of wild laughter, but that erupts through a frame of strongly asserted artistic order which simultaneously reflects a view of social behaviour as moves in a game ordered by conventions, unrecognised by most of the players but apparent, within limits, to the adroit. The relationship of artistic and social orders is made manifest in the symbolic game of chess which provides a horribly witty comment on the crucial seduction of act II. That, by making apparent the stylization inherent in social activity, marks the transition from the naturalism of I.i towards the manifest stylization of act V.

Dramatic naturalism is, of course, always relative. Middleton's city comedies, especially the brilliant *A Chaste Maid in Cheapside*, were always stylized; but they made their stylization out of an acutely observed imitation of behaviour and language in the London they represent. They use, for this, a great deal of prose, and so, in the comic plot, does *The Changeling*. *Women Beware Women* uses prose very rarely, almost exclusively in the ward's scenes to mark his distinctive idiocy, a mental (not social) lower order that can never be completely assimilated to the formal dance and so will eventually (by mis-timing, a failure of rhythm) fatally destroy his guardian's masque and his guardian with it. Otherwise the play is entirely in verse, which is made to establish a basic norm for the language within which relatively slight shifts can transform, for instance, Leantio's naive cupidity into Fabritio's grave legalism or Hippolito's erotic idealism. The language of I.i. , though generally common in vocabulary, is not that really used by such people, except in occasional colloquial phrases. What makes it distinctively Leantio's own is his constant preoccupation with possession, his engaging self-satisfaction with both profit and affection which are associated from his first words:

Mother.   What's this gentlewoman?

Leantio. Oh you have named the most unvalued'st
                                                                 purchase
That youth of man had ever knowledge of.
As often as I look upon that treasure,
And know it to be mine — there lies the blessing —
It joys me that I ever was ordained
To have a being, and to live 'mongst men ...

                                                  (I.i.11–17)

The complacence is marvellously done, and links perfectly with sheer acquisitive possession:

                          'tis theft, but noble
As ever greatness yet shot up withal.

Mother. How's that?

Leantio.   Never to be repented, Mother,
Though sin be death; I had died, if I had not sinned.
And here's my masterpiece: do you now behold her!
Look on her well, she's mine.   (37–42)

The cosiness is amazing and dominates the scene, although the traps are carefully pointed:

Mother.   Y'are to blame,
    If your obedience will give way to a check,
    To wrong such a perfection.

Leantio.   How?

Mother.   Such a creature,
    To draw her from her fortune—which no doubt,
    At the full time, might have proved rich and noble—
    You know not what you have done.   (56–61)

Less directly, Bianca suggests the limits of the sexual
satisfaction as well as of the economic:

    Kind Mother, there is nothing can be wanting
    To her that does enjoy all her desires.
    Heaven send a quiet peace with this man's love,
    And I am as rich as virtue can be poor ... (125–8)

It will be no surprise to find her desires going beyond
Leantio in both.

The domestic cocoon embraces scene i; scene ii displays
the same complacence, but the critical exposure is
considerably sharper. It starts, pertinently, by calling our
attention to language in Guardiano's commentary on
Fabritio's legal-commercial vocabulary:

                    If now this daughter
    So tendered (let me come to your own phrase, sir)
    Should offer to refuse him, I were hanselled.
    [*Aside*] Thus am I fain to calculate all my words
    For the meridian of a foolish old man,
    To take his understanding.

                                (I.ii.8–13)

Livia is more direct with Fabritio's assumption of absolute
control over his daughter's choice in marriage:

    Maids should both see, and like; all little enough;
    If they love truly after that, 'tis well.
    Counting the time, she takes one man till death,
    That's a hard task, I tell you. But one may

Enquire at three years' end amongst young wives
And mark how the game goes.

Fabritio.   Why, is not man
  Tied to the same observance, lady sister,
  And in one woman?   (32–9)

She answers him with a pertinent definition of the double
standard:

                              'Tis enough for him;
  Besides he tastes of many sundry dishes
  That we poor wretches never lay our lips to:
  As obedience forsooth, subjection, duty, and such
                                            kickshaws,
  All of our making, but served in to them.
  And if we lick a finger then sometimes,
  We are not to blame; your best cooks use it. (39–45)

Livia's wit maintains an acute social observation – that
obedience, subjection and duty are made *by* women but
offered *to* men – across her more obviously bawdy
suggestions, the 'many sundry dishes' men enjoy, and the
'lick a finger then sometimes' with which women respond.
Livia's witty, bawdy, common sense suggests a latter-day
Wife of Bath, and the association is made fairly explicit:

Fabritio. Th'art a sweet lady, sister, and a witty —

Livia. A witty! Oh the bud of commendation
  Fit for a girl of sixteen; I am blown, man,
  I should be wise by this time; and for instance,
  I have buried my two husbands in good fashion,
  And never mean more to marry.

Guardiano.   No, why so, lady?

Livia. Because the third shall never bury me.
  I think I am more than witty; how think you, sir?
                                              (46–53)

The number of husbands is more modest than in Chaucer,

but there is a hint that she may lick a finger sometimes and, at her own will, exercise a freedom the Wife of Bath did not consider.

Commerce and sex both become more sharply, and more dangerously, defined before act I is over. The exposition shifts first to Fabritio's daughter Isabella and his brother Hippolito. Their intimacy is announced with innocent approval:

> *Fabritio.* Those two are ne'er asunder; they've been heard
>   In argument at midnight, moonshine nights
>   Are noondays with them ...
>
> *Guardiano.*   Oh affinity,
>   What piece of excellent workmanship art thou!
>   'Tis work clean wrought, for there's no lust, but love
>   in't,
>   And that abundantly; when in stranger things
>   There is no love at all, but what lust brings. (63–73)

The change of tone pronounces a higher respect for them, and their intimacy is also a sensitive, intelligent resistance to the world of Fabritio. The contrast is made sharply clear when Guardiano's ward appears: an idiot, a childish mind in an adult body, oscillating between pride in his skill with his cat-stick, and boasting of his lust. Hippolito and the ward are in total contrast, and Isabella has no rational choice to make. The idea that she should love this clot is absurd, as Livia tells Fabritio; he sees it, but still commands the marriage. Left alone, Hippolito and Isabella speak their feelings to the audience, but not to each other. They are both driven by the external pressure, he to declaring his incestuous love, she to despair at a woman's subjection, whether from her father's will or, as she recognises, by her own choice:

> Men buy their slaves, but women buy their masters.
>   (176)

Encouraged by their shared distress, Hippolito comes to

explicit declaration, and that drives Isabella to shocked rejection:

Hippolito. I love thee dearlier than an uncle can.

Isabella. Why so you ever said, and I believed it.

Hippolito. ...
As a man loves his wife so love I thee.

Isabella. What's that? Methought I heard ill news come
                                                    toward me,
Which commonly we understand too soon,
Then over-quick at hearing. I'll prevent it ...
                    What's become
Of truth in love, if such we cannot trust —
When blood that should be love is mixed with lust?
                                        (211–227)

Act I is completed by the first hint of an equivalent blasting of the cosy world of Leantio: his job as factor (merchant's agent, a kind of commercial traveller) requires his absence, and he struggles successfully against his own uxoriousness and Bianca's pleadings. But as soon as he has gone, his mother is reminded that the Duke's procession is due to pass their house, so she and Bianca watch from a window. Their commentary betrays nothing, but hints everything in its reticence:

Mother. How like you, daughter?

Bianca.   'Tis a noble State.
Methinks my soul could dwell upon the reverence
Of such a solemn and most worthy custom.
Did not the Duke look up? Methought he saw us.

Mother. That's ev'ry one's conceit that sees a duke;
If he look steadfastly, he looks straight at them;
When he perhaps, good careful gentleman,
Never minds any, but the look he casts
Is at his own intentions, and his object
Only the public good.

Bianca.   Most likely so.

Mother. Come, come, we'll end this argument below.
Exeunt.
(I.iii.102–112)

Act I has established with rare fullness a bourgeois
commercial environment; by the end it has looked above
that to the superior sensibilities of Hippolito and Isabella,
linked together by 'affinity', not merely in the sense of
blood relationship but also in their common feeling of
repudiating their background; finally it looks 'above' in a
different sense, with Bianca, to the wealth and splendour
(and lust) of the Duke. The whole structure of the play is
predicated in these developments. Act II is entirely located
in Livia's house. Strictly, this is no higher in the social scale
than her brother Fabritio's, but it emerges as a link place,
where citizen and courtier meet. In scene ii Livia entertains
the widow, Leantio's mother, and doing so, rather
obviously patronises her, protesting an easy friendship that
the widow finds it hard to respond to; and here, at the
same time, the Duke can visit her. He is, certainly, intent
on whoring and treats Livia and Guardiano as convenient
bawds, the house as a private brothel; but that impression
exaggerates a social situation which Middleton establishes
with characteristic precision. In act III Livia's house is a
location where the Duke can be publicly entertained to
dinner, bringing Bianca with him now as his established
mistress; it is perhaps implicit that he could not do this
elsewhere, but at the same time there is no effort to keep
the occasion secret. By act IV Bianca has moved into the
Duke's palace and is attended there by two ladies; but as
she is still merely his mistress the pair are subject to the
Cardinal's magnificent denunciation. By the end of the act
Leantio has been murdered and the Duke finally marries
her, only to receive another high rebuke from his brother.
In act V she shares the throne room with her husband, and
in the grand masque to celebrate their wedding they all
die.

This is, certainly, Bianca's rise in the social scale, but it is also the play's; locations are clearly indicated, and they change by acts: I is in mercantile Florence, first Leantio's house, then in Fabritio's; II and III are both in Livia's house; IV is in the private apartments of the Duke, and V is in the state room. The relation of cast to environment changes appropriately, and equally gradually. Fabritio and the widow are left behind after act III, but Leantio is cynically hoisted into the court world by his highly improbable appointment as Captain of the fort at Rouans—a palpable device to buy the husband's complicity. Livia, Guardiano, Hippolito and Isabella can all retain a presence in act IV, but they enter the state room of act V only as masquers to entertain the nobility, not as guests at the aristocratic feast. The ward is there, too, but he is usefully as well as symbolically placed below stairs (to work the trap-door). These people are, by this time, literally out-classed, and their performance loses assurance: the sheer incompetence which makes the masquing murders so wildly farcical is at least partly a function of their social displacement—a highly sophisticated version of the rustic bungling of court entertainment in *Love's Labour's Lost* and *A Midsummer Night's Dream.*

The dominant mores shift with the social location. The opening scenes are the essence of the bourgeois, and the final scene is equally essentially aristocratic, court masque and all. Between the two Bianca is, certainly, 'corrupted', but corruption is hardly the exclusive perquisite of the court; indeed, corruption is not really the right word: Middleton does not offer the distinct preference for bourgeois domesticity that Webster seems to do. There is a simple charm in Leantio's pride in his stolen wife, and in Bianca's physical affection for him:

You have not bid me welcome since I came.

Leantio. That I did questionless.

Bianca. No sure, how was 't?
I have quite forgot it.

Leantio.   Thus.   [*Leantio kisses her.*]

Bianca.   Oh sir, 'tis true,
   Now I remember well. I have done thee wrong,
   Pray take 't again, sir.   [*They kiss again.*]
                                         (I.i.142–6)

But, as I showed, that affection is indissolubly linked with
commercial ambition. Leantio reflects on his profession:

   Though my own care and my rich master's trust
   Lay their commands both on my factorship,
   This day and night I'll know no other business
   But her and her dear welcome. 'Tis a bitterness
   To think upon tomorrow: that I must
   Leave her still to the sweet hopes of the week's end,
   That pleasure should be so restrained and curbed,
   After the course of a rich workmaster
   That never pays till Saturday night.   (151–9)

So he comes to the conclusion which his background
naturally proposes:

   Who could imagine now a gem were kept
   Of that great value under this plain roof?
   But how in times of absence? What assurance
   Of this restraint then? Yes, yes, there's one with her:
   Old mothers know the world, and such as these,
   When sons lock chests, are good to look to keys.
                                         (171–6)

The widow's good sense can see the danger of her son's
elopement, but it cannot quite manage the total in-
carceration of her daughter-in-law. She enjoys the show of
the Duke's passing, and is not too difficult to tempt round
to Livia's house. Leantio has a comfortable domestic ethic,
but his absolute is possession which he cannot impose on
his wife, nor even on his mother.

   At the other end of the play, the court has its own
interfusion of flexible and absolute mores. The Duke's will
is paramount, and his will is to have Bianca, on any terms

that may become necessary. He wants her at once as
desired object and as image of perfect beauty:

> Come, Bianca,
> Of purpose sent into the world to show
> Perfection once in woman; I'll believe
> Henceforward they have ev'ry one a soul too
> 'Gainst all the uncourteous opinions
> That man's uncivil rudeness ever held of 'em.
> Glory of Florence, light into mine arms!
>
> (III.iii.22–8)

It is obvious that he is trangressing a taboo, although he
can recreate it proudly as 'man's uncivil rudeness'. The
moral attitude implied here has the splendour of absoluteness, and it is given much more direct expression by his
brother, the Cardinal:

> But, great man,
> Ev'ry sin thou commit'st shows like a flame
> Upon a mountain, 'tis seen far about,
> And with a big wind made of popular breath
> The sparkles fly through cities—here one takes,
> Another catches there, and in short time
> Waste all to cinders.
>
> (IV.i.207–213)

That, he says, 'your reason grants'; he extends his
argument into the immanence of death:

> Think upon 't, brother; can you come so near it,
> For a fair strumpet's love? And fall into
> A torment that knows neither end nor bottom
> For beauty but the deepness of a skin,
> And that not of their own neither? Is she a thing
> Whom sickness dare not visit, or age look on,
> Or death resist? Does the worm shun her grave?
> If not, as your soul knows it, why should lust
> Bring man to lasting pain, for rotten dust?
>
> (243–251)

The Duke submits, but only so far as not to sleep with Bianca again until he has married her, and he finds even that delay difficult:

> She lies alone tonight for 't, and must still,
> Though it be hard to conquer; but I have vowed
> Never to know her as a strumpet more,
> And I must save my oath. If fury fail not
> Her husband dies tonight, or at the most
> Lives not to see the morning spent tomorrow;
> Then will I make her lawfully mine own,
> Without this sin and horror.   (267–274)

Absolute morality, resisted by lust, begets murder as blindly here as it did with Beatrice-Joanna, in the amazing claim that they can then sleep together 'Without this sin and horror'.

Lust, then, plays the devil with moral systems as widely different as the factor's and the Duke's. In between, a pivot between them, is the flexible mores that Livia presides over, far more sophisticated than Leantio's and without the public magnificence of the Duke's. Its tone is instantly established in II.i as Livia moves to resolve the frustration of her favourite brother, Hippolito. At first she attacks him:

>   Is the world
> So populous in women, and creation
> So prodigal in beauty and so various,
> Yet does love turn thy point to thine own blood?
> 'Tis somewhat too unkindly.
>   (II.i.4–8)

But she quickly turns round:

>   'tis but a hazarding
> Of grace and virtue, and I can bring forth
> As pleasant fruits as sensuality wishes
> In all her teeming longings. This I can do. (29–32)

So she can, simply by hazarding truth: she persuades Isabella that she was a bastard whom her mother discreetly passed off as Fabritio's, keeping her secret until a death-bed confession; and she persuades her too that respect for her mother's memory demands that even Hippolito shall not be told.

So Isabella goes to Hippolito's bed as if it were the incest which in truth it is. Livia is embarked on a course she conducts with professional pride, but some secret unease:

> This 'tis to grow so liberal — y' have few sisters
> That love their brothers' ease 'bove their own
>   honesties,
> But if you question my affections,
> That will be found my fault.   (70–73)

This initiates a characteristic pattern in Middleton: sin breeds sin. Livia proceeds to extend her bawdy activities in collusion with her 'sojourner' (lodger), Guardiano, as far as procuring the hidden young gentlewoman, Bianca, for the Duke. She does it with a delightful mixture of wit and bawdy delight, backed by an explicit female resistance to the prevailing male domination:

> A thing most happily motioned of that gentleman,
> Whom I request you, for his care and pity
> To honour and reward with your acquaintance:
> A gentleman that ladies' rights stands for,
> That's his profession. ...
> Come, widow. [*To Bianca*] Look you, lady, here's our
>   business. [*Pointing to the 'Table and Chess'*]
> Are we not well employed, think you? An old
>   quarrel
> Between us, that will never be at an end.
>
> *Bianca.* No, and methinks there's men enough to part
>   you, lady.
>
> *Livia.* Ho! but they set us on, let us come off
> As well as we can, poor souls, men care no farther.
>   (II.ii.254–267)

The game of seduction is played out like the chess game in a beautifully organised scene. Livia and the widow play their game on the main stage while Guardiano takes Bianca up to the gallery (here literally 'above') to see the pictures, so that the Duke can emerge there and seduce her. The commentary is therefore a series of *double entendres*:

Livia. Alas, poor widow, I shall be too hard for thee.

Mother. Y'are cunning at the game, I'll be sworn, madam.

Livia. It will be found so, ere I give you over.
  She that can place her man well —

Mother.   As you do, madam.

Livia. As I shall, wench, can never lose her game
                                        (294–8)

The widow's short-sightedness makes her even confuse the black and white men; she can see nothing at all of the encounter above. The joke, bawdily entertaining, is also nastily at the expense of the widow's simplicity – 'blind' in more than one sense:

Livia. Did not I say my duke would fetch you over, widow?

Mother. I think you spoke in earnest when you said it, madam.

Livia. And my black king makes all the haste he can too.

Mother. Well, madam, we may meet with him in time yet.

Livia. I have given thee blind mate twice.

Mother.   You may see, madam,
  My eyes begin to fail.

Livia.   I'll swear they do, wench.
                                        (388–393)

The mother always addresses Livia as 'madam', while Livia responds with 'wench' which marks the patronising superiority she affects to deny.

When Bianca returns from the bedroom she is at first appalled:

> Now bless me from a blasting; I saw that now
> Fearful for any woman's eye to look on.
> Infectious mists and mildews hang at 's eyes,
> The weather of a doomsday dwells upon him.
>
> (420–423)

and she articulates the basic moral in a violent rebuke to Guardiano:

> Murders piled up upon a guilty spirit
> At his last breath will not lie heavier
> Than this betraying act upon thy conscience.
> Beware of off'ring the first-fruits to sin:
> His weight is deadly, who commits with strumpets
> After they have been abased, and made for use ...
>
> (431–6)

But once she comes forward to the other players she readily adopts the double talk to her mother-in-law:

> *Mother.* You have not seen all since sure?
>
> *Bianca.*   That have I, Mother,
> The Monument and all. I'm so beholding
> To this kind, honest, courteous gentleman,
> You'd little think it, Mother, showed me all,
> Had me from place to place, so fashionably—
> The kindness of some people, how 't exceeds!
> 'Faith, I have seen that I little thought to see,
> I' th' morning when I rose.   (450–457)

The laughter of the scene is akin to Flamineo's in its accurate and cynical perception, but here it is not located in a given speaker, it is constructed for the audience in the elaborate staging of the scene itself.

In act III Bianca's tone has shifted to violently frustrated shrewishness at her imprisonment which bewilders the mother, and Leantio too when he returns from his business trip. Livia's pleasure in life has produced a valid contempt for 'grace and virtue' as they emerge in conventional or systematic moralities; it produces also emotional and physical frustration. Bianca must have the Duke and, as the widow foresaw in act I, she must have his wealth as well. Livia, importantly for the balance of perception here, needs no more wealth than her husbands have bequeathed her; but she does need a lover and finds him, inappropriately enough, in the dispossessed Leantio. For him it is a kind of revenge, and an attempt to live a more sophisticated life, to 'keep up with' Bianca. Livia does not need, or have, illusions about him or the depth of his feeling for her, but she is nonetheless bitterly hurt when he is murdered. The Duke, understanding that Hippolito has an extreme pride in the reputation of his family, reveals the relationship to him, and Hippolito takes the expected (and certainly very ungrateful) revenge. So Livia reveals her original deception to Isabella who is appalled to know that her love is indeed incestuous. The plot enacts the moral logic with quite rare precision.

As much as Livia's house provides a staging-post in the social 'rise' of the play from factor's home to ducal court, and in the corresponding gradations of mores, so also it is a stage in a progression of dramatic modes. The play, like *Romeo and Juliet*, is always geared explicitly towards tragedy but enacts that through a succession of changing forms of comedy. Act I draws vividly on Middleton's experience in city comedy; acts II and III advance that towards what is usually called 'high comedy', the sophisticated wit that engages the audience with double talk above the heads of some of the cast, and therefore potentially of some of the audience – Leantio and his mother, and their social counterparts. Running through both these phases is the antibody, social, moral, and dramatic, of the Ward. He is a fool, whose witless crudity is the base matter out of which all cultivated socio-moral worlds are developed; or, to put it another way, over which they are all thin veneers. He wants to play games, shuttlecock and battledore chiefly, but directly sexual games as well, and he makes no bones about it. He's crudely funny, and pathetic as well, and he can therefore be used to expose human weaknesses that finer tones and verse will always tend to cover up: (he and his servant are discussing the match with Isabella)

Sordido. These are the faults that will not make her pass.

Ward. And if I spy not these, I am a rank ass.

Sordido. Nay more: by right, sir, you should see her naked,
 For that's the ancient order.

Ward. See her naked?
 That were good sport, i' faith. I'll have the books turned over,
 And if I find her naked on record,
 She shall not have a rag on. But stay, stay,
 How if she should desire to see me so too? I were in a sweet case then, such a foul skin.

(II.ii.117–125)

Which, of course, is true too, and not merely of the Ward, behind all the fine sentiments and fine clothes. To see that, to see the Fool, is to see the implication of farce that is latent in the whole play; and it is that which emerges simultaneously with the grand tragic climax in act V.

Indeed the tragic climax *here* precisely is farcical. Bianca's attempt to kill the hostile Cardinal which misfires onto her husband, Isabella's revenge on Livia and Livia's on Hippolito, Guardiano's last show of stage-managing – all are achieved in court masquing of gloriously amateur incompetence: every plan goes wrong, but they all die just the same. The dearth of stage directions in the original text makes the action singularly obscure, and

even the careful additions made by the *Revels* editor are
not enough to serve the reader or help a stage director very
much. Confusion is indicated by the Duke's efforts to
follow the action by reading the 'plot' which he has been
given:

> But soft! here's no such persons in the argument
> (V.ii.65)

he remarks of the first brief masque; indeed there are not,
because Bianca has interpolated her little piece before
Guardiano's main show begins. That is not its only puzzle:
Hymen gives her cup satisfactorily to Bianca, but Hebe
and Ganymede trip over each other and deliver theirs into
the wrong hands—so the Duke drinks the poison intended
for the Cardinal and, because it is a slow poison (by stage
standards), Bianca doesn't realise what has happened until
the main masque is over. Whether the audience should
ever get it clear I am not sure. Hebe and Ganymede
accuse each other of stealing wine in clumsy impromptu
couplets which seem to be part of their masque:

> Take heed of stumbling more, look to your way;
> Remember still the Via Lact-e-a.   (59–60)

That is an obscure allusion, as the notes point out, to the
myth of Hebe stumbling with Jove's nectar and so creating
the milky way; but the obvious joke is that the 'milk' was
actually wine, and Hebe retorts:

> Well, Ganymede, you have more faults, though not
>   so known;
> I spilled one cup, but you have filched many a one.
>   (61–2)

It seems the young ladies are drunk, and is strongly
reminiscent of the proceedings when James I entertained
his father-in-law the king of Denmark and one courtly
nymph fell into Christian's lap while another had to be
helped outside to vomit on the stairs (1). Hymen hastily
ushers her disorderly charges out.

There is no suggestion of drunkenness in the cast of the main masque. There the confusions spring from the deaths that are not in the plot but essential in the plotting: that is, the device breeds its own disaster. Isabella infects Livia, suspended on high as the matronly Juno, with poisoned smoke, and Livia, realising she is dying ('This savour overcomes me' 114), hurls flaming gold at Isabella who dies at once. 'This', as the Duke observes, 'swerves a little from the argument though' (123), and the designed climax goes awry. The Ward has been planted below the stage to work the trap when Guardiano stamps above, and he has been carefully warned against mistiming:

> If this should any way miscarry now,
> As, if the fool be nimble enough, 'tis certain ...
>
> (V.i.30–31)

so it is mysterious why, when Guardiano does stamp, it is he himself who immediately falls through (to die on spikes below). It would be obvious to assume that it is the Ward's fault, but it is not clear how it can be. My best guess is that as Hippolito dances forward toward the trap he sees that Isabella is actually dead and breaks step to go to her, and so Guardiano, seeing this, also breaks step and so lands on the trap himself. However it is arranged, the rhythm of the dance is broken and it becomes the joke of the engineer hoist with his own petard that Marlowe had used at the end of *The Jew of Malta*. But Livia is too far-seeing to have left this to chance and so has her Cupids fire poisoned arrows at Hippolito who, crouching over Isabella, is now a sitting target. The poison is not instantaneous and he has time for an impressively dignified speech of explanation before running on the guard's halbert and so accelerating his death into the form of a noble suicide. But even that dignity is deflated by a lord's inane comment (reminiscent of the lords at the end of *The Duchess of Malfi*):

> Behold, my lord,
> 'Has run his breast upon a weapon's point.
>
> (V.ii.168–9)

The audience must have seen that already, and so must
laugh at the words.

The whole of that sequence is bridged by the slow
working of Bianca's poison. She continues to expect the
Cardinal's death and only understands when the Duke
begins to fail. With him, of course, her hopes must end, so
finally she voices her despair and finishes the cup herself
before the Cardinal can stop her. Her final speeches are
quietly effective enough to quell the wild laughter:

> Now do; 'tis done.
> Leantio, now I feel the breach of marriage
> At my heart-breaking. Oh the deadly snares
> That women set for women, without pity
> Either to soul or honour! Learn by me
> To know your foes; in this belief I die:
> Like our own sex, we have no enemy, no enemy!
>
> (209–215)

That is moving; what it does not have, which briefly the
end of *The Changeling* did, is any echo of the imaginative
glimpse of hell so characteristic of the wild laughter in
Tourneur and Webster.

Masque uses dance in movement as it uses lyric verse in
language, and the actuality of death is felt as a jarring of
the formal rhythm of the dance. That is Middleton's
achievement in the last movement of his play. The
progression from naturalism to stylization ends there: it has
passed from the solid domesticity of act I, through the
identification of the moves of the game, to the elaborate
but strictly amateur rituals of court entertainment. This
process accompanies the other progressions I have identified, of comedy through high comedy to tragi-farce, and
of bourgeoisie through *haute bourgeoisie* to aristocracy, and
from factor's mores through sophisticated free-thinking to
courtly absolutes of honour and rectitude. All those
patterns, with remarkable verbal intricacy, echo each other
in the play's development. They control the seeming

development from giving any first fruits to sin into the final disaster: I say seeming because the court mores are not strictly more corrupt than Leantio's, but they are grander, being absolute, and therefore more fatal. Nowhere in drama is the proposition that tragedy belongs to persons of high rank given more thorough, or more ambiguous, expression. In all the plays considered in this book, moral rectitude has been associated, if anywhere, with middle class traditions: Vindice's sister, Vittoria's mother, the Duchess's own marriage, even in *The Changeling* with Isabella, though Middleton does not offer a preference so clear as Webster's. Tragedy develops from association with great men and women whose grandeur is far more aesthetic than moral. The logical conclusion of *Women Beware Women* is developed directly out of the factor's muddled world. That perception resists the simplified moral which Bianca offers; so do countless counter-perceptions that constantly come from mouths not credited with moral authority (as the Cardinal should be), such as Bianca's comment on repressive education in act IV:

> 'tis not good, in sadness,
> To keep a maid so strict in her young days;
> Restraint breeds wandering thoughts, as many fasting
> days
> A great desire to see flesh stirring again.
> I'll ne'er use any girl of mine so strictly:
> Howe'er they're kept, their fortunes find 'em out;
> I see 't in me: if they be got in court,
> I'll never forbid 'em the country, nor the court,
> Though they be born i' th' country; they will come
> to 't
> And fetch their falls a thousand mile about,
> Where one would little think on 't.
>
> (IV.i.30–40)

Private flexibility is given positive as well as negative value, and there is at least as much conviction in that statement as in the spectacle of an inevitable progress of sin to tragedy.

Middleton is far too intelligent a moralist to rest on anything so simple. His lack of simple conviction has brought on him, again and again, the charge of ultimate cynicism which is, I think, absurd. His is the subtlest moral intelligence of the Jacobeans. He was also, I think, the most controlled artist. And in this play, even more than in *The Changeling*, he demonstrates the absurdity of worshipping tragedy as a moral force: it is exposed as being as morally dangerous as it is artistically perfect. Its beauty depends on moral absolutes, and the hostility of aesthetic to tenable moral values animates the laughter that attends its climax.

VII

'Tis Pity She's A Whore

All the plays in this book show awareness of each other, which is at least partly why they make such a clear sequence and seem to constitute their own genre; they show too, of course, awareness of Shakespeare's work, especially of *Romeo and Juliet, Hamlet,* and (less specifically) *Othello.* Ford, more than anyone else, uses these models obviously, even blatantly; but he does not seem to invite his audience to be conscious of his borrowings as allusions, he uses what he takes to create his own play. *'Tis Pity She's a Whore* is as difficult to date as Middleton's tragedies, so strictly speaking we do not know who borrowed from whom, but at least it is clear that the connection was close. The play has elements that relate it to both *The Changeling* and *Women Beware Women,* and since they appear in Ford's play somewhat like transferable units less precisely integrated than in Middleton's I find myself assuming that he wrote later; but it may not have been so: the relationship is certainly more interesting than the sequence and the difference is worth noting as a difference in dramatic structure.

'Tis Pity is set, like Middleton's tragedies (and like *Romeo and Juliet*), in a small Italian city state, and the incest theme is made to depend on social isolation; but although in one way Ford seems to assert this symbolic significance of

incest by making it central, he also seems to be much less interested in social context than Middleton. Florio excites the aristocrat Soranzo's contempt because he is a merchant, but the point is incidental here and the mercantile values are not explored. Annabella does not lack alternative suitors, she is not (apparently) exceptionally young, and the sight of men is not for her a brave new world. Although she is nothing like a whore, her creation owes more to Bianca than to Beatrice-Joanna, and even that is only directly noticeable in one scene, IV.iii, when her cruelly contemptuous retorts to the violently jealous Soranzo clearly echo Bianca's shrewish behaviour to her mother-in-law and husband after she has become the Duke's mistress:

> *Soranzo.*   Excellent quean!
>   Why, art thou not with child?
>
> *Annabella.*   What needs all this,
>   When 'tis superfluous? I confess I am.
>
> *Soranzo.* Tell me by whom.
>
> *Annabella.*   Soft, sir, 'twas not in my bargain.
>   Yet somewhat, sir, to stay your longing stomach
>   I'm content t' acquaint you with: the man,
>   The more than man that got this sprightly boy —
>   For 'tis a boy, that for your glory, sir,
>   Your heir shall be a son —
>
> *Soranzo.*   Damnable monster!
>   (IV.iii.25–33)

But again the context has been radically changed: Middleton exposes social frustration in the narrow domestic environment whereas in Ford there is scarcely any social distinction between husband and lover-brother (and no stress on it at all), and the language functions simply as contempt for the *man* who is, to Annabella, inferior. Soranzo is established as Giovanni's inferior for a reason that is not social at all: he lacks intellectual distinction, and his romanticism is limited by his masculine double-standard, his dangerously arrogant treatment of his cast-off adultery with Hippolita.

Intellectual romanticism thus becomes isolated as the glory on which the play depends, and to which all its distinct elements are related; it is expressed, not by Annabella primarily, but by Giovanni. And it is in Giovanni, rather than in her, that exceptional inexperience is stressed as a pre-condition for tragic behaviour. He has been isolated, not so much by his small town background, as by his academic concentration, as his father notes:

> And he is so devoted to his book,
> As I must tell you true, I doubt his health ...
>
> (I.iii.5–6)

In the last act he is called mad by several actors but it is not the simple insanity of Cordelia (or Ophelia) nor even the wolvish deterioration of Ferdinand, it resembles rather the manic sanity of Kyd's Hieronimo, a single-minded devotion to an action at odds with all social norms. If, that is to say, Giovanni is strictly mad at all: nothing suggests that he is so clinically and his extra-ordinariness consists in the perfection of an intellectual and emotional aesthetic. 'Love' is an ideal, normally divided between family and sexual relations which are as likely to conflict as to complement each other. The consequent confusion leads to familiar forms of compromise, and Giovanni resolves the dilemma by uniting both:

> Say that we had one father, say one womb
> (Curse to my joys!) gave both us life and birth;
> Are we not therefore each to other bound
> So much the more by nature? by the links
> Of blood, of reason? nay, if you will have 't,
> Even of religion, to be ever one,
> One soul, one flesh, one love, one heart, one *all*?
>
> (I.i.28–34)

That is what makes incest the symbolic as well as the

dramatic centre of the play. The ideal concepts of Love unite here in intellectual perfection. Something of this perception is visible in Hippolito's affair with Isabella in *Women Beware Women*, although Middleton laid more stress on psychological compulsion than intellectual appreciation, for superiority to their family is felt in these terms. Ford makes them the centre of the tragedy, and so gives tragedy a distinctive aesthetic glory. If it is mad, it is mad only in the sense that perfection is always and necessarily mad.

Middleton's aesthetic was, in *Women Beware Women*, primarily a matter of dramatic stylization, the masque as ultimate commentary on the social realities in which his play began. Webster's, on the other hand, stressed the strange forms of visual beauty which drama can create. Ford's is more distinctively intellectual than either, not so much because it is philosophical as because it elevates an abstract Idea distinct from the personal sexual relationship for which Ford also writes brilliantly. An evident corollary is, with Giovanni, a superb contempt for moral and social conventions perceived as 'common sense':

> Busy opinion is an idle fool,
> That, as a school-rod keeps a child in awe,
> Frights the unexperienced temper of the mind.
> So did it me; who ere my precious sister
> Was married, thought all taste of love would die
> In such a contract: but I find no change
> Of pleasure in this formal law of sports.
>
> (V.iii.1–7)

Giovanni's superiority appears as an aristocratic tone, but its origin is not a matter of social rank. Soranzo is the aristocrat of the play and is marrying beneath him in marrying Annabella since Florio is apparently a merchant and his pride is certainly that he is rich. What distinguishes Giovanni is his intellect. He makes his incestuous affair into a conceptual glory and so the play has a dimension which was hardly positive in the others I have discussed.

Grand passion is present in both Webster and Middleton, but it is always presented too equivocally to carry dominant conviction. It is equivocal with Giovanni, certainly, but the beauty of the concept is now central to the play's structure, where it will remain, for better or for worse, throughout the subsequent development of seventeenth century tragedy. Ford owes something to Beaumont and Fletcher in this, and at least as much to Chapman, whose *Bussy D'Ambois* is echoed in several scenes (1). From Chapman comes the intellectual stress and, with Chapman's acknowledged master Marlowe, the association of intellectual individualism with atheism. But with them intellectual freedom, however ambivalently perceived, was a profoundly serious pursuit; Ford clearly understands that, but if he was committed to it his play hardly shows the commitment. Marlowe and Chapman were both dramatists, but in both we feel some involvement of author with hero; we do not feel that with Ford. The equivocal response to incest (beauty/disgust) partly functions as an emblem of the equivocal response established to 'heroic love'.

It is necessary to get this clear, for it is what makes Ford's drama distinctive. In his later plays, *The Broken Heart* in particular, it is almost the whole play and develops the conflict of absolute virtue with absolute love that is equally characteristic of Corneille and most of later heroic drama in England as in France. But in *'Tis Pity* it is still located, as Clifford Leech demonstrated (2), in a context that is distinctively Jacobean. The play's exceptionally numerous sub-plots form an anthology of motifs from earlier work, and all involve laughter in various forms, much of it bawdy. Annabella's 'tutor', Putana, is an old bawd, but she is obviously a version of Juliet's nurse with a hearty affirmation of the necessity of sex coupled with easy acceptance of irregular behaviour:

> Then he is bountiful; besides he is handsome, and, by
> my troth, I think wholesome—and that's news in a

> gallant of three and twenty. Liberal, that I know;
> loving, that you know; and a man sure, else he could
> never ha' purchased such a good name with Hippolita
> the lusty widow in her husband's lifetime—and
> 'twere but for that report, sweetheart, would a were
> thine! Commend a man for his qualities, but take a
> husband as he is a plain-sufficient, naked man ...
>
> (I.ii.91–9)

Soranzo is a promising husband because he is not known
to have syphilis and because his virility is attested by his
notorious affair with Hippolita. Putana's tolerant humour
might provide an alternative view of the main characters'
behaviour, a version of the comic world of *The Changeling*,
but Ford sticks closer to Juliet's nurse and Putana functions
ultimately rather as a dangerous blindness:

> Nay, what a paradise of joy have you passed under!
> Why, now I commend thee, charge; fear nothing,
> sweetheart, what though he be your brother? Your
> brother's a man I hope, and I say still, if a young
> wench feel the fit upon her, let her take anybody,
> father or brother, all is one.
>
> *Annabella.* I would not have it known for all the world.
>
> *Putana.* Nor I indeed, for the speech of the people; else
> 'twere nothing.
>
> (II.i.45–52)

Gossip, the speech of the people, does destroy the lovers;
but so does the thing itself.

Putana is not directly an agent in any plot, and even her
status as tutor does not seem to give her more than
marginal influence over Annabella: we hardly take
seriously the proposition that her readiness for incest might
derive from such an Overdone education. Vasques, her
male counterpart, is more sinister and more involved. He
figures in the main plot as Soranzo's servant who both
restrains his master's fury and feeds it by identifying his

enemy for him. He is also involved in the quarrel with
Grimaldi, and much more fully with Hippolita's attempted
revenge. In all of these he appears to be faithful to Soranzo,
but fidelity is hardly his motive. His malice obviously
derives from Iago and so, no doubt, does his inscrutability.
He restrains Soranzo only to control his revenge, so he also
inflames his jealousy:

> Am I to be believed now? First, marry a strumpet that
> cast herself away upon you but to laugh at your
> horns? To feast on your disgrace, riot in your
> vexations, cuckold you in your bride-bed, waste your
> estate upon panders and bawds?
>
> *Soranzo.* No more, I say no more!
>
> *Vasques.* A cuckold is a goodly tame beast, my lord.
>
> *Soranzo.* I am resolved ...
>
> (V.ii.1–8)

He can also be cynically informative about sexual
behaviour, in a tone which differs only slightly from
Putana's:

> She is your wife; what faults hath been done by her
> before she married you, were not against you; alas
> poor lady, what hath she committed, which any lady
> in Italy in the like case would not?
>
> (IV.iii.81–4)

But his jokeyness covers a strange and disturbing pretence
of loyalties that never become convincing, and from which
an absolute detachment occasionally emerges, sometimes
violently. He teases and flatters Putana into revealing
Annabella's affair with Giovanni, plausibly insinuating his
own and even Soranzo's tolerance of the way of the world;
but when she tells him what he wants to know, he
instantly summons his comic banditti to take her off to the
coal-shed and put her eyes out. It's a horrid eruption, of
which there are few in the play, and Putana never

reappears which makes it almost inconsequential.

Inconsequential is, I think, the right word for all the sub-plots, even when they come closest to the centre. They all bear on the main plot, but none ever quite touches it. Vasques' other engagement is with Hippolita, the virago whose passion exposes Soranzo's shabby masculinity and turns to passionate revenge. She engages Vasques as accomplice, bribing him with both her wealth and her bed, and plans a climax in a wedding masque that is strongly reminiscent of Bianca's impromptu show in *Women Beware Women*. Hippolita's plan, like Bianca's, miscarries and the grotesque fantasy becomes partly farcical in her isolated absurdity. But it does not miscarry because of drunken accident: Vasques deliberately perverts it so that Hippolita, not Soranzo, drinks the poison and dies, and no-one on stage knows that he has done it. The audience does know, but not in advance: we are given no fore-knowledge. It can, consequently, be taken in the choric words of the stage audience as 'Wonderful justice' (IV.i.88), but the cosmic moral is ironic: Vasques is his own, not Providence's, agent. The scene therefore invites sardonic laughter though it is never as farcical as Middleton's.

'Wonderful justice' is clearly placed as ironic; so, but more obscurely, are all the explicit morals of the play. The Cardinal has the last word, as cardinals should, and he has not been represented as so hopelessly corrupt as Webster's are; he is, in fact, more like Middleton's, except that he represents an arrogant and evidently detestable papal authority. First, when he protects Grimaldi from the consequences of his blatant murder (hardly mitigated by the fact that he accidentally killed the wrong man):

> Rise up, Grimaldi.
> You citizens of Parma, if you seek
> For justice: know, as Nuncio from the Pope,
> For this offence I here receive Grimaldi
> Into his Holiness' protection.
> He is no common man, but nobly born;

Of princes' blood, though you, sir Florio,
Thought him too mean a husband for your daughter.
If more you seek for, you must go to Rome,
For he shall thither; learn more wit, for shame.
Bury your dead. —Away, Grimaldi; leave 'em.

(III.ix.52–62)

And again in act V, in case we should forget what he is, he extends Vasques' treatment of Putana:

Peace! First, this woman, chief in these effects,
My sentence is that forthwith she be ta'en
Out of the city, for example's sake,
There to be burnt to ashes.

(V.vi.132–5)

He then banishes Vasques and finally delivers the compassionate moral of the play. But in between, very briefly, he has associated himself with another moral voice as Richardetto throws off his disguise as doctor and emerges for the first time in the play in his own person (he is Hippolita's husband, believed to be dead):

Richardetto. Your grace's pardon: thus long I lived
                                                    disguised
    To see the effect of pride and lust at once
    Brought both to shameful ends.
Cardinal. What, Richardetto, whom we thought for
                                              dead? (151–4)

Richardetto's piety emerged as his wife died – 'Heaven, thou art righteous' and 'Here's the end/Of lust and pride' (IV.i.88 and 101–2) – and the irony then was patent, since his presence in the play is to seek revenge on her and on Soranzo. Thus, at the end, when Soranzo also has died without his help, Richardetto can unmask and join the moral chorus. But it is patently an equivocal chorus, composed of Vasques, Cardinal and Richardetto. The friar might have done better: he is ineffectual, but he is not discredited. As it is, the proper moral comments are weakened by being uttered since they are uttered by doubtful voices. The effect is much like the end of Marlowe's *The Jew of Malta* where the Christian Governor belatedly refers his Machiavellian victory to heaven.

Richardetto is altogether a strange figure. He is supposed to have died at sea and until the very last lines of the play remains disguised as a doctor; indeed he does not hesitate to perform professionally when Annabella is taken ill, with the result that he does not realise she is pregnant which Putana sees at once. His primary purpose is revenge on Soranzo and he does get as far as suborning Grimaldi, but when that goes awry he seems to take no further action. Most of his time is taken up with his niece, Philotis, who seems light-heartedly to fall in with all his schemes, including marriage with the fool Bergetto. This links them positively to a comic world, and Philotis cheerfully accepts her part in that:

> *Richardetto.*   My lovely niece, you have bethought 'ee?
>
> *Philotis.* Yes, and as you counselled,
>   Fashioned my heart to love him, but he swears
>   He will tonight be married; for he fears
>   His uncle else, if he should know the drift,
>   Will hinder all, and call his coz to shrift.
>   (III.v.26–31)

Philotis's couplets parody the poetic form of Giovanni's declaration of love in I.ii, itself an echo of the sonnet in which Romeo and Juliet celebrate their first meeting:

> *Giovanni.*   The poets feign, I read,
>   That Juno for her forehead did exceed
>   All other goddesses; but I durst swear
>   Your forehead exceeds hers, as hers did theirs.
>
> *Annabella.* Troth, this is pretty!

Giovanni.   Such a pair of stars
  As are thine eyes would, like Promethean fire,
  If gently glanced, give life to senseless stones.

Annabella. Fie upon 'ee!

Giovanni. The lily and the rose, most sweetly strange,
  Upon your dimpled cheeks do strive for change.
  Such lips would tempt a saint; such hands as those
  Would make an anchorite lascivious.

Annabella. D'ee mock me, or flatter me?

(I.ii.192–204)

Annabella treats that as a joke, and Giovanni might well play it with some witty self-awareness, but he is certainly also serious. Philotis is not serious, but she is engagingly honest: she is in no way deceived about Bergetto, but if she takes him on she will do it with affection, and if her grief at his death is obviously not profound it is really more remarkable that it is grief at all. Such cool emotion, that is still emotion, functions as effective contrast both to the destructive passion of her aunt Hippolita and to the intense glory of Annabella's love and Giovanni's. With Philotis, comedy has some of the same value that it has, on a larger scale, with Isabella in *The Changeling*.

Bergetto and his uncle-guardian Donado are almost identical with the Ward and Guardiano in *Women Beware Women* in relationship, language, and specific details, even to the absurd letter the idiots insist on writing for themselves in a form which is at once deliberately and accidentally bawdy. Bergetto has at least a naive directness: he wants to get his bauble in somewhere, into Annabella if she'll have him (which of course she won't), if not a whore will do as well:

Donado. Well sir, now you are free, you need not care
  for sending letters now: you are dismissed, your
  mistress here will none of you.

> *Bergetto*. No? why, what care I for that; I can have
>   wenches enough in Parma for half-a-crown apiece,
>   cannot I, Poggio?
>
> *Poggio*. I'll warrant you sir.
>
> (II.vi.108–114)

Bergetto the idiot is evidently the opposite of Giovanni the
intellectual lover: hero and fool are foils to each other, and
their deaths are effectively contrasted. Bergetto's end
comes in act III, and in several respects it echoes Mercutio's
death in act III of *Romeo and Juliet*. It is purely accidental,
and the fact that it is fatal is only slowly recognised; an
entirely comic reaction is gradually understood to be a
pathetic, and very touching, disaster:

> *Bergetto*. O help, help, here's a stitch fallen in my guts;
>   O for a flesh-tailor quickly!—Poggio!
>
> *Philotis*. What ails my love?
>
> *Bergetto*. I am sure I cannot piss forward and backward,
>   and yet I am wet before and behind; lights, lights, ho
>   lights!
>
> *Philotis*. Alas, some villain here has slain my love!
>
> *Richardetto*. O, Heaven forbid it! Raise up the next
>   neighbours
>   Instantly, Poggio, and bring lights.   *Exit* Poggio.
>   How is 't, Bergetto? slain? It cannot be;
>   Are you sure y' are hurt?
>
> *Bergetto*. O, my belly seethes like a porridge-pot; some
>   cold water, I shall boil over else. My whole body is in
>   a sweat, that you may wring my shirt; feel here—
>   why, Poggio!   . . .
>
> *Richardetto*. Tear off thy linen, coz, to stop his wounds;
>   Be of good comfort, man.
>
> *Bergetto*. Is all this mine own blood? nay then, goodnight
>   with me; Poggio, commend me to my uncle, dost

hear? Bid him for my sake make much of this
wench — O, I am going the wrong way sure, my
belly aches so — O, farewell, Poggio — O — O — *Dies.*

Philotis. O, he is dead!

Poggio.   How! dead?

Richardetto.   He's dead indeed.
  'Tis now too late to weep; let's have him home,
  And with what speed we may find out the murderer.

Poggio. O my master, my master, my master!   *Exeunt.*
                                    (III.vii.8–37)

Laughter at Bergetto's death is silenced in somewhat
bemused pathos. With Giovanni's end the indications are
less clear, but the process seems to be the opposite. The
long erotic bed scene in which he kills Annabella depends
on their being both aware that exposure is immanent:

Annabella. Brother, dear brother, know what I have
                                    been,
  And know that now there's but a dining-time
  'Twixt us and our confusion . . .
                                    (V.v.16–18)

Giovanni does not kill her simply because he is jealous of
her repentance, her new 'honesty' to her husband, but
because a suicide pact is their only logical conclusion:
tragedy is an aesthetic of death. But his jealousy spoils his
concept of the act:

                         why, I hold fate
  Clasped in my fist, and could command the course
  Of time's eternal motion; hadst thou been
  One thought more steady than an ebbing sea.
  And what? You'll now be honest, that's resolved?
                                    (11–15)

Like Othello, he is afraid that his sacrifice may become a
common murder:

> *Stabs her.*
>
>   Thus die, and die by me, and by my hand:
>   Revenge is mine; honour doth love command.
>
> *Annabella.* O brother, by your hand?
>
> *Giovanni.*   When thou art dead
>   I'll give my reasons for 't; for to dispute
>   With thy—even in thy death—most lovely beauty,
>   Would make me stagger to perform this act
>   Which I most glory in.   (85–91)

That glory becomes what he calls his 'last and greater
part' (106), his celebrated entry to the final banquet with
Annabella's heart upon his dagger. It is a magnificent
shock, and one that concentrates the positive and negative
polarities of Ford's drama. It can be seen as symbolising the
ultimate emotional defiance to which Giovanni has always
aspired, the perfect climax of love as death; but it is also, in
being that, the act of blind destruction, the ultimate
exposure of the deathly pursuit of absolutes; yet again, it
can also be seen as playing a part, a merely histrionic
gesture, perfectly absurd. The conjunction in this shock of
horror, emotional satisfaction, and derisive laughter is a
brilliant but difficult climax, and it presents problems in
staging. It can be done with a sheep's heart dripping real
blood, which makes the horror apparent, but if it is taken
so literally it is apt to be too small to be clearly
recognisable enough for its symbolic value to register. If, as
is sometimes done, a large cardboard heart is used, the
symbolic point is clear but the shocking actuality is lost.
The solution must partly depend on the size of auditorium
that the effect must reach, but to recognise the problem is
at least to see the ambiguity of response demanded. That is
amplified in the ambiguity of the word 'mad' applied to
Giovanni afterwards, and all aspects of the response find a
place in the language used. The emotional intensity of

> My sister, O my sister!   (V.vi.20)

transposes into the grand claim:

> The glory of my deed
> Darkened the mid-day sun, made noon as night.
> $$(21-2)$$

But that, extended brilliantly, does tend towards becoming overtly insane:

> You came to feast, my lords, with dainty fare;
> I came to feast too, but I digged for food
> In a much richer mine than gold or stone
> Of any value balanced: 'tis a heart,
> A heart my lords, in which is mine entombed.   (23–7)

A sudden shift into colloquialism marks the maniacal glee:

> Look well upon 't; d'ee know 't?

> *Vasques.* What strange riddle's this?

> *Giovanni.* 'Tis Annabella's heart, 'tis; why d'ee startle?
> I vow 'tis hers: this dagger's point ploughed up
> Her fruitful womb . . .   (28–32)

Giovanni is not answering Vasques but himself: his self-absorption carries his own rhythm straight on. Laughter is implicit here, but neither Giovanni, nor the scene, decomposes into *mere* laughter: as Florio voices the suspicion 'Why, madman, art thyself?' Giovanni's utterance recovers its dignity and he can convincingly reply 'Yes father' (34–5).

The scene usually does provoke laughter, and the play's intelligence requires that. But that laughter depends at the same time precisely on the aesthetic perfection which the laughter must attack, and if that perfection is not genuinely admired the structure will simply collapse. Ford writes brilliantly in the major scenes for Giovanni and Annabella, at once movingly and beautifully; his work is poetical in a sense that Middleton's never was, and the Revels editor,

Derek Roper, may be justified in claiming of Ford's verse
that 'its musical and emotional effects are sometimes gained
at the expense of meaning, which is thinned down or
evacuated' (Introduction, pp. xlvi–vii). Those scenes need
to be excellent, for the play's structure depends on them. It
depends, in fact, on an aesthetic concept about which it is
seriously ambivalent. Annabella is emotionally convincing
in a variety of modes: love, sexuality, even bawdy humour
as they enter from bed at the beginning of act II:

> *Giovanni.* I marvel why the chaster of your sex
> Should think this pretty toy called maidenhead
> So strange a loss, when being lost, 'tis nothing,
> And you are still the same.
>
> *Annabella.*   'Tis well for you;
> Now you can talk.
>
> *Giovanni.*   Music as well consists
> In th' ear, as in the playing.
>
> *Annabella.*   O, y' are wanton!
> Tell on 't, y' are best, do.
>
> *Giovanni.*   Thou wilt chide me, then?
> Kiss me, so; thus hung Jove on Leda's neck,
> And sucked divine ambrosia from her lips.
> I envy not the mightiest man alive,
> But hold myself in being king of thee
> More great, than were I king of all the world.
> But I shall lose you, sweetheart.
>
> *Annabella.*   But you shall not.
>
> *Giovanni.* You must be married, mistress.
>
> *Annabella.*   Yes, to whom?
>
> *Giovanni.* Someone must have you.
>
> *Annabella.*   You must.
>
> *Giovanni.*   Nay, some other.

Annabella. Now prithee do not speak so without jesting;
> You'll make me weep in earnest.

(II.i.9–25)

She is dignified in handling Soranzo's unwelcome wooing,
and brilliant in defiant scorn when he discovers her
pregnancy; finally, she is moving in passionate repentance:

> That man, that blessed friar,
> Who joined in ceremonial knot my hand
> To him whose wife I now am, told me oft
> I trod the path to death, and showed me how.
> But they who sleep in lethargies of lust
> Hug their confusion, making Heaven unjust,
> And so did I.

(V.i.24–30)

What Isabella does not share with Giovanni is his
conceptual absolutism. He makes his idea depend on an
abstract fate because it has nothing to do with moral,
religious or social norms, but whenever he uses the word it
is in a context of self-justification, and therefore not wholly
credited:

> Or I must speak, or burst; 'tis not, I know,
> My lust, but 'tis my fate that leads me on.

(I.ii.158–9)

Ford's play rests, then, on a structure of ideas which we
are not required to share. An aesthetic of tragedy which is
at once beautiful and ridiculous. And that, no doubt, is
why it is set amidst such numerous and confusing motifs so
clearly (and so ably) borrowed from other plays. Ford's
sub-plots are, even by Jacobean standards, exceptionally
confusing, and this is only partly because there are so many
of them. It is primarily because they almost all fail, and
having not come off, merely fade away so that irrelevance
comes to seem their characteristic. The sheer incompetence
of Hippolita, Richardetto, Grimaldi lead to the pathetic
farce of Bergetto's death. Their bustling variety has, no

doubt, contributed a world of familiar dramatic life, but in the end it seems principally to have acted as foil to the brilliant clarity of the central action, and the reiterated irrelevance becomes a conductor to drain off potentially distracting modes of moral or social judgement. In the sub-plots Ford owes most to Middleton, but I agree with Derek Roper (Introduction, p. l, n.2) that he uses what he takes without generating anything like the same interest in social actuality.

It follows that the play's laughter is not so wildly disturbing as Tourneur's or Webster's, nor as morally serious as Middleton's. Yet it is still essential, for the play centres on an intellectual idea of tragedy that is perceived as at once beautiful and absurd; for that, incest is the perfect matter since it was, and (perhaps uniquely) still is, a socio-sexual taboo of unquestioned absoluteness, which yet has no clear rational origin. In later plays Ford related his aesthetics to positive celebration of ideal aristocratic virtues of Honour and Love that neither required nor could endure laughter. It is ultimately that shift in the social reference of the drama as well as the accompanying shift in aesthetic which terminates the line of plays considered in this book. Ford, borrowing so much from Middleton, recognised in *'Tis Pity* the moral perversity that is inherent in the beauty of tragedy, and he borrowed therefore the laughter that attends his climax: but he gives far more stress than Middleton did to the aesthetic glory. That accompanied the Caroline revival of aristocratic absolute mores, and the derisive laughter died in later plays–until the Puritan efforts to close the theatres in the 1640s coincided with the final tragedy of Stuart apotheosis in the theatrical dignity of Charles I on the scaffold. As Marvell has it in the Horatian Ode:

> *He* nothing common did or mean
> Upon that memorable scene.

★   ★   ★

I have distinguished in the course of discussing these six plays a number of different *qualities* of laughter: the light gaiety of the Duchess with Antonio; the good-humoured comedy of Isabella and her suitors; the crude folly of the Ward and Bergetto; the broad shared joke that Vindice sometimes offered, or Flamineo occasionally; the more penetrating cynical wit of 'I have caught/An everlasting cold' or 'Why then,/Your credit's sav'd' or 'A woman dipp'd in blood, and talk of modesty?'; the wholly mirthless laughter, like cannon, 'The Lord Ferdinand laughs'. Beyond them there is the cynical joke verging on hysteria to which Vindice inclines: 'be merry, merry,/Advance thee, O thou terror to fat folks' or 'Nine coaches waiting,—hurry, hurry, hurry' which verges on the savage strangeness of Ferdinand's 'I'll go hunt the badger, by owl-light'. The list could be refined and the examples multiplied, but I have deliberately refrained from any attempt at formal classification because I think it would only distort the range and flexibility with which all forms of laughter here bear on one another. For they are all subject to their context in tragic violence, in a way that is typified by the madmen who dance before the Duchess's death and speak bawdy jokes in the grotesque context of madness, torture, death. The different qualities of laughter respond differently, of course, to the context: the Duchess's gaiety transposes through hideous shock into pathos; Ferdinand's mirthlessness into violent insanity; Isabella's sane comedy illuminates the insanity of Beatrice, Alsemero or De Flores' satisfaction with the hell-fire that consumes Diaphanta. And the context, equally, responds differently to them. It is that complex interaction where laughter and tears are both opposite and identical (whether an audience laughs or not it must always be conscious of both) which constitutes these plays' distinctive achievement, their most penetrating image of the Death-in-Life they all study. There is no doubt in this case that he who laughs last laughs best, for that is always death, the skull that Vindice carried from the opening of the play.

Wild laughter resists order, and diminishes the neat social and even cosmic orders to which the plays appeal. The weakness of the statements of order-restored which they offer – the last words of Giovanni in *The White Devil* are a good example – is that the sardonic humour of such as Flamineo lives after them. *He* voiced it, and his character matched the voice; but analysis of that character is not a definitive analysis of the laughter. The character is founded on social dispossession and personal resentment; the laughter attacks order, celebrates anarchy, generates chaos: it is, therefore, at once destructive and creative. It is the laughter of much of *Hamlet*, of all of *The Revenger's Tragedy*, and of much of the rest of these plays. It cannot be unequivocally valued, morally or metaphysically; it is tragic laughter. These plays are properly known as tragedies, but only if their horrid laughter is realised as essential to their tragic form. They are of the theatre theatrical, and it is from that that they derive their shared experience; together they constitute a group of extra-ordinary distinction which, together with the comedies of Jonson and Middleton, should, after Shakespeare, be recognised as the core of our classical repertory. Marlowe could join them, and a small handful of Restoration comedies, notably Wycherley's; beyond that there has been great English drama in the theatre but few if any great texts to feed it.

Notes

Chapter I, p. 1, n. 1:
>S. Freud (ed. J. Strachey): *Jokes and their Relation to the Unconscious* (New York, 1960); H. Bergson, 'Laughter', in W. Sypher (ed.): *Comedy* (New York, 1956).

p. 7, n. 2:
>The most enlightening account of this is still A. P. Rossiter, *English Drama from Early Times to the Elizabethans* (London, 1950).

Chapter II, p. 10, n. 1:
>See L. Salingar, *'The Revenger's Tragedy* and the Morality Tradition', *Scrutiny* VI (1937-8), 402-24, and R. Ornstein, *The Moral Vision of Jacobean Tragedy* (Madison, Wis., 1965).

Chapter III, p. 29, n. 1:
>See M. Curtis, 'The Alienated Intellectuals of Early Stuart England', *Past and Present* 23 (1963), 25-43; L. Stone, 'The Educational Revolution in England, 1560-1640', *Past and Present* 28 (1964), 75-7; V. Morgan, 'Cambridge University and "The Country" 1560-1640', in L. Stone (ed.): *The University in Society* (Princeton, New Jersey, 1974), vol. I, 235.

p. 30, n. 2:   See below, p. 68.

Chapter IV, p. 56, n. 1:
>I.-S. Ekeblad (Ewbank), ' "The Impure Art" of John Webster', *Review of English Studies* N.S.9 (1958), 253–67.

p. 68, n. 2:
>I.-S. Ewbank, 'Webster's Realism or, "A Cunning Piece Wrought Perspective" ', in B. Morris (ed.): *John Webster* (Mermaid Critical Commentaries, London, 1970), 157–178.

Chapter V, p. 72, n. 1:
> See my *Shakespeare's Early Tragedies* (London, 1968), 81–3.

Chapter VI, p. 106, n. 1:
> Reprinted in R. Ashton (ed.): *James I by his Contemporaries* (London, 1969), 242–4.

Chapter VII, p. 115, n. 1:
> E.g. II.i, the lovers returning from bed, echoes the same situation in *Bussy D'Ambois* II.i; and in IV.iii, Soranzo's jealous fury and determination to identify the offender is closely based on Montsurry's jealousy of Tamyra in V.i.

p. 115, n. 2:
> *John Ford and the Drama of his Time* (London, 1957), 41–64.

Suggestions for Further Reading

Editions
The best are in *The Revels Plays* (see Preface); others are available in *The Regents Renaissance Drama Series,* and *The Mermaid Series.*

Reference
G. E. Bentley: *The Jacobean and Caroline Stage,* 7 vols. (Oxford, 1941-68)
S. Wells (ed.): *English Drama, Excluding Shakespeare* (Select Bibliographical Guides) (London, 1975)

General
H. Bergson, 'Laughter', in W. Sypher (ed.): *Comedy* (Madison, Wis., 1965)
S. Freud (ed. J. Strachey): *Jokes and their Relation to the Unconscious* (New York, 1960)
T. S. Eliot: *Selected Essays* (London, 1932)
M. C. Bradbrook: *Themes and Conventions of Elizabethan Tragedy* (Cambridge, 1935)
U. Ellis-Fermor: *The Jacobean Drama: An Interpretation* (London, 1936)
A. Kernan: *The Cankered Muse: Satire of the English Renaissance* (New Haven, Conn., 1959)
J. R. Brown & B. Harris (eds.): *Jacobean Theatre* (Stratford-upon-Avon Studies) (London, 1960)
R. Ornstein: *The Moral Vision of Jacobean Tragedy* (Madison, Wis., 1960)
I. Ribner: *Jacobean Tragedy: The Quest for Moral Order* (London, 1962)
R. B. Heilman: *Tragedy and Melodrama: Versions of Experience* (Seattle, Wash. and London, 1968)
D. L. Frost: *The School of Shakespeare* (Cambridge, 1968)
R. Levin: *The Multiple Plot in English Renaissance Drama* (Chicago, Ill., 1971)

Tourneur

L. G. Salingar, '*The Revenger's Tragedy* and the Morality Tradition', *Scrutiny* 6 (1937-8), 402–24

I. Ekeblad (Ewbank), 'An Approach to Tourneur's Imagery', *The Modern Language Review* 54 (1959), 489–98

P. B. Murray: *A Study of Cyril Tourneur* (Philadelphia, Pa., 1964)

B. J. Layman, 'Tourneur's Artificial Noon: The Design of *The Revenger's Tragedy*', *Modern Language Quarterly* 34 (1973), 20–35

J. A. Barish, 'The True and False Families of *The Revenger's Tragedy*', in S. Henning, R. Kimbrough, R. Knowles (eds.): *English Renaissance Drama* (Carbondale, Ill., and London, 1976)

S. Wells, '*The Revenger's Tragedy* Revisited', in G. R. Hibbard (ed.): *The Elizabethan Theatre* VI (Waterloo, Ont., 1976)

Webster

T. Bogard: *The Tragic Satire of John Webster* (Berkeley and Los Angeles, Cal., 1955)

I. Ekeblad (Ewbank), 'Webster's Constructional Rhythm', *ELH* 24 (1957), 165–76

'"The Impure Art" of John Webster', *Review of English Studies* N.S.9 (1958), 235–67

C. Leech: *Webster: The Duchess of Malfi* (Studies in English Literature) (London, 1963)

N. Rabkin (ed.): *The Duchess of Malfi* (Twentieth Century Interpretations) (Englewood Cliffs, N.J., 1968)

G. K. & S. K. Hunter (eds.): *John Webster: A Critical Anthology* (Harmondsworth, 1969)

B. Morris (ed.): *John Webster* (Mermaid Critical Anthologies) (London, 1970)

D. C. Gunby: *The White Devil* (Studies in English Literature) (London, 1971)

R. Berry: *The Art of John Webster* (Oxford, 1972)

A. Dalby: *The Anatomy of Evil: A Study of John Webster's The White Devil* (Lund, 1974)

R. V. Holdsworth (ed.): *Webster,* The White Devil *and* The Duchess of Malfi: *A Casebook* (London, 1975)

L. Potter, 'Realism Versus Nightmare: Problems of Staging *The Duchess of Malfi*', in J. G. Price (ed.): *The Triple Bond: Plays, Mainly Shakespearean, in Performance* (Pennsylvania, 1975)

R. F. Whitman, 'The Moral Paradox of Webster's Tragedy', *P. M. L. A.* 90 (1975), 894–903

M. B. Charney, 'Webster Versus Middleton, or the Shakespearean Yardstick in Jacobean Tragedy', in S. Henning, R. Kimbrough, R. Knowles (eds.): *English Renaissance Drama* (Carbondale, Ill. and London, 1976)

Middleton

W. Empson: *Some Versions of Pastoral* (London, 1935)

S. Schoenbaum: *Middleton's Tragedies: A Critical Study* (New York, 1955)

G. R. Hibbard, 'The Tragedies of Thomas Middleton and the Decadence of the Drama', *University of Nottingham Renaissance and Modern Studies* 1 (1957)

R. H. Barker: *Thomas Middleton* (New York, 1958)

C. Ricks, 'The Moral and Poetic Structure of *The Changeling*', *Essays in Criticism* 10 (1960), 290–306

'Word-Play in *Women Beware Women*', *Review of English Studies* N.S.12 (1961), 238–50

E. Engleberg, 'Tragic Blindness in *The Changeling* and *Women Beware Women*', *Modern Language Quarterly* 23 (1962), 20–28

J. B. Batchelor, 'The Pattern of *Women Beware Women*', *Yearbook of English Studies* 2 (1972), 78–88

D. M. Farr: *Thomas Middleton and the Drama of Realism: Representative Plays* (Edinburgh, 1973)

Ford

C. Leech: *John Ford and the Drama of His Time* (London, 1957)

M. Stavig: *John Ford and the Traditional Moral Order* (Madison, Wis., 1968)

D. K. Anderson: *John Ford* (New York, 1972)